The Way to Write and Publish a Cookbook

THE WAY TO WRITE AND PUBLISH A COOKBOOK

DORIS McFERRAN TOWNSEND

ST. MARTIN'S PRESS · NEW YORK

Design by Laura Hough

Library of Congress Cataloging in Publication Data

Townsend, Doris McFerran.
The way to write and publish a cookbook.

1. Cookery—Authorship. I. Title.
TX644.T68 1985 808'.066641 84-23795
ISBN 0-312-85836-1
ISBN 0-312-85837-X (pbk.)

Contents

Chapter Four
OLD-PRO TECHNIQUES: WRITING NONRECIPE MATERIAL 87

The body of the book—importance of section titles and introductions. Getting across need-to-know information. Surrounding the body—front matter and back matter: what they consist of, how to approach them. Preliminary index work, with pep talk and cautionary notes.

Chapter Five
ASSAULT ON THE CITADEL: SELLING YOUR BOOK 103

Researching publishers—the rifle, rather than the scattergun, approach saves time and effort. Where and how to look for the right publisher for your book. Vanity presses, self-publishing, agents: pros and cons. The query—what to write, what to send. Publishers are people; if you approach them with that in mind, they'll respond in kind.

Chapter Six
A CONSUMMATION DEVOUTLY TO BE WISH'D: THE SOLD BOOK 126

Try, try again must be the writer's philosophy. What to do when you try and fail, when you try and succeed. Money matters—advances, royalties, flat fees, writer-for-hire circumstances. How to read and understand a publisher's contract; traps to avoid, including the "satisfactory manuscript" clause. Revising, checking copy-editing, reading proof.

Chapter Seven
MIXED BAG: ADVERTISING, PROMOTION, PERKS, FREEBIES, AND OTHER MATTERS 162

There's more to writing a book than simply putting words on paper. Selling your book to the public—what you can do to help, what the publisher does (or ought to do). Making the most of every opportunity.

Chapter Eight
SPECIAL CIRCUMSTANCES: COMMUNITY AND FUND-RAISER COOKBOOKS 188

A special kind of self-publishing—by committee. How to get organized. Staff, finances, work plans. Calling for and handling recipes; testing, editing. Finding a printer. Making arrangements to sell the book to the public. Will you make a profit?

Chapter Nine
ORNAMENTAL FROSTING: FOOD-PHOTOGRAPHY SESSIONS 218

How cookbooks are illustrated. Who creates the pictures, who pays for them. Photographers, cooks, home economists, stylists, and other special breeds. Props, sets, and other special needs—including lunch.

A Library for Cookbookers 240

Index 248

The Way to Write and Publish a Cookbook

Chapter One
Cookbookery: It's a Big Business

When I was eight or nine years old, my father asked me what I wanted to be when I grew up. After a little thought (this was long ago, in the time of Bonnie and Clyde, Scarface Al, and John Dillinger), I replied that I'd like to become a gangster's moll. Falling from the lips of his innocent child, this so flummoxed Dad that he didn't bring up the subject again for more than two years. When he did I informed him, to his patent relief, that I wanted to be a writer and produced as evidence twelve school notebooks comprising a novel I had recently finished. Its title was *Georgianna and the U.S. Males.* In spite of that, the concept so pleased—or, at least, relieved—my father that he promptly converted a small room in our house to an office for me, complete with desk, swivel chair, file cabinets, typewriter, and red leather chair for "sitting and thinking." (The result of this grandeur was a crippling five-year case of writer's block, but that's another story.)

The point is that when you ask a group of youngsters about their goals in adult life, you'll doubtless get the usual "nurse" and "fireman" and "actor." Perhaps even a "writer" or two. But I'll bet the royalties from my most recent book that not one, male or female, will answer "cookbook author." Why?

Because no one ever seems to aim at being a writer of cookbooks. It's an accidental, fall-into sort of profession. Nevertheless, a great number of people, writers and nonwriters from all walks of life, do fall into it. It's a clean, respectable, pleasant way to make a living, far superior to, for example, ditch digging or bank robbing, and certainly less dangerous. And although fortunes are seldom made in the cookbook business, a comfortable living can be, provided you have something worth saying and know the accepted, professional way to say it.

This comes as a surprise—and sometimes an affront—to writers in other fields, but cookbooks sell very well. Indeed, until recently they outsold all categories of books other than the Bible. But a couple of years ago, romance novels nudged cookbooks out of second place. Not surprising, when you think about it. The cover blurb on a romance novel presently on sale promises readers "Unbridled desire, untrammeled lust, in a steamy jungle atmosphere redolent of frangipani." How can a book offering Original Boston Baked Beans and Aunt Lulu's Special Spice Cake, in a steamy kitchen atmosphere redolent of fried fish, hope to compete?

WHO WRITES COOKBOOKS?

Sooner or later just about everyone—or at least just about everyone who cooks—at least thinks about writing a cookbook. This is particularly true of those whose friends say, as they push themselves back from the dinner table, "That was a great meal—you ought to write a cookbook."

It's not all that simple. Being a dynamite cook helps, but it's not the entire answer. In the first place, cookbooking is not nearly as much fun as cooking. It requires organizational skills, writing skills, and an abundance of patience. It requires inventiveness, creativity. You need to understand something of the chemistry of cooking: why cakes rise (or fall), why if a certain amount of butter produces an excellent result twice as much is not better, why a week-old egg is better to hard-cook than a fresh-laid one, and literally hundreds more such morsels of knowledge. More important, you must want to know these things, feel the need to know them; you must fall on each new little nugget that comes your way with shouts of joy and a sense of having improved yourself.

You do need to be a good cook, but not necessarily a great one. If your success in the kitchen rests solely on the ability to read a recipe and follow directions, plus a lot of panache, you aren't necessarily qualified. You must also constantly—as you cook, as you read cookbooks, as you leaf through magazines, as you dine in a restaurant or at a friend's house—ask yourself questions. What would happen if I used brown sugar here instead of white? Would lamb with yogurt instead of beef with sour cream make a good stroganoff-type dish? Was it solely egg whites that gave this dessert its texture or was a bit of gelatin added? You must be willing to experiment. And you must be willing to pick yourself up and abide by the instructions of the old saying "If at first you don't succeed. . . ."

Amateur writer-cooks often get into cookbooking because they have in their possession material that seems worthy of print. It might be a body of recipes handed down from Great-aunt Sophia, reputed to have been a smashing cook. Or someone perhaps comes upon the neatly hand-printed kitchen instructions of a class of people known for their culinary talents, such as the Shakers, the Society of Viennese Pastry Workers, or the chefs at Delmonico's who so pleased the gluttonous palate of Diamond Jim Brady. Such a treasure makes a great starting point—makes, in fact, cookbook authors of people who never before wrote anything other than letters to their boyfriends in boot camp.

Writers who are professionals in other fields often turn to cookbookery. Travel writers, for example, see and sample so many different kinds of food that they can't help talking about them, and finally decide that they might as well talk on paper and make some money while they're at it. Other professionals sometimes get into the business by so simple a back door as a publisher friend's call for help with a mass of interesting but presently unpublishable material that has come in. Or they may be asked for assistance—for a fee or a share of the royalties—by a nonwriter who has cookbook material but neither the time nor the expertise to make it into a book.

Celebrities, too, write cookbooks, although more often than not these are ghosted by food-oriented professionals. Sometimes, though, the actor, singer, comedian, or whatever manages the feat on his own—and quite nicely, thank you. A number of years ago, Vincent Price, the suave and handsome actor whose forte is scaring us witless, produced, with the collaboration of his wife, a handsome and very good cookbook, *A Treasury of Great Recipes,* that is still in demand. But generally a celebrity cookbook is put together by some nameless drudge who is paid a flat fee. If by chance the book takes off, the glory and the royalties are garnered by the celebrity.

Professionals in the food business account for a great number of the cookbooks that appear each year. Home economists top the list, particularly those whose profession is originating, developing, and testing recipes for food companies, food trade associations, and public-relations firms and advertising agencies that deal with food companies. Food writers and editors who work for magazines, newspapers, PR companies, and food-related programs for radio and television are also likely to get into cookbooking, either as a sideline or as a full-time occupation. So are the many people who work in food illustration as stylists or cooks for the looks-too-good-to-eat photographs that appear in magazines and newspapers, on TV, in advertisements, and on food packages. Chefs, sous-chefs, cooks, and caterers—and, for all I know, scullions and dishwashers—put their professional association with food to good secondary use by writing cookbooks. So do the proprietors of food-vending establishments, from the elegant *charcuterie-boulangerie-pâtisserie* shops that have recently sprung up far and wide to the smallest cookies-by-mail enterprise. Many of these people have baccalaureate and graduate degrees in home economics or have studied at one of the fine restaurant and hotel management schools. On the other hand, many hold degrees in some subject totally unrelated to food, or have no degrees at all—as we mentioned before, the food business is a great fall-into occupation.

If you have a flair for cookbookery and the time and patience to treat it as a job rather than as a nice little hobby, don't be dismayed by the credentials of the competition. Just bear in mind that, as is true of any other writer, a cookbook author must have the ability to put together interesting, well-constructed, grammatically correct sentences and assemble them into an inviting, readable, cohesive text. (Publishing houses have editors who will, in theory, do that for you, but in practice you will have great difficulty catching the eye—not to mention the respect—of an editor if you lack the basic writing skills.) So, no matter what your professional credentials or lack of them, if you are ready, willing, and able, go ahead and write a cookbook.

WHO BUYS (OR BEGS, BORROWS, OR STEALS) COOKBOOKS?

Gift givers constitute a large class of book buyers, and cookbooks command their share of the purchases. Cookbooks make admirable gifts for the soon-to-be-married, brides, upwardly mobile home cooks who are bent on improving their meals as well as their image, and practically anyone who enjoys time spent in the kitchen. (However, for those who feel that the perfect gift for a cookbook author is another cookbook, one word of advice: Don't! Too many people have already had the same idea. Not only that, but each of the author's friends who has written a cookbook has thoughtfully sent along a complimentary copy. Likewise, friends in the publishing business automatically send hot-off-the-press copies of their newest offerings. Most cookbook authors are up to their armpits in cookbooks and sinking fast.) The only one to whom a cookbook may not come as a pleasant surprise is the helpless, hopeless cook who can't boil water without burning it and longs for someone to invent a viable substitute for the alimentary canal.

A substantial number of cookbooks are bought by people who read them as others read novels, savoring each moment, devouring every page, breathing heavily at the denouement, shedding a furtive tear as they come to the end, eagerly looking ahead to the next offering by the same author. Some of these are abstainers, who wouldn't dream of eating all the goodies they read about; many abstainers, constantly dieting and constantly hungry, use cookbooks as a kind of substitution therapy, a way of having their cake but not eating it too. Some cookbook readers can't cook worth a nickel. Some are gourmets, some gourmands, some your basic pig-outers. Some are so-so cooks who fantasize cooking their way through the book they are reading as others fantasize being left a million dollars by a hitherto unknown uncle. Whatever their motives, reading cookbooks is their fix, a buffer between them and the travail of the everyday world, their ticket to never-never land.

By far the largest number of cookbook buyers, however, are the users. They are the practical ones who know their own abilities and limitations and cook accordingly from carefully chosen cookbooks that serve them well. Some of these are experimenters, looking to hone their skills, upgrade their output, and expand their culinary horizons. These are the most fun to write for, and the most appreciative audience for your efforts.

LOOKING AT COOKBOOKS FROM ALL SIDES

It is possible to categorize cookbooks in a number of ways, depending on the point you want to make. One is by physical properties. Broadly, there are hardcover and softcover books. The former range from simple books limited in their physical dimensions (or what is known as "trim size") and number of pages, without illustrations, to big, thick, handsomely produced books lavishly illustrated with full-color photography. Softcover books may be the sort that leap to mind when we say the word "paperback"—small of dimension, printed in relatively small type on relatively cheap paper. They are perfect bound, which means that the pages are glued rather than sewn to the spine—and also means, unfortunately, that the books will not lie flat when open unless you break the backs, after which the pages are likely to fall away like leaves in autumn. They are seldom illustrated, and virtually never in color unless a few pages of coated stock—a higher-grade paper—are bound in to carry the pictures. There is another sort of paperback, sometimes called "deluxe" but known to the publishing business as the "trade" paperback, of a larger trim size, printed in more legible type on better paper, and usually illustrated in color; this style of paperback is often used by publishing houses specializing in books—how-tos, fix-its, gardening guides, repair manuals, cookbooks—that cry out for illustration.

There are also cookbooks with special bindings: comb bindings made of plastic and wire-o bindings that are formed of a long spiral of wire are two of these. Generally they are used because, although they are more expensive than perfect bindings, they are less expensive than sewn hardcover bindings, and have the great advantage of allowing the book to lie flat when open. There are also fancy ring bindings, like gussied-up school notebooks, with washable covers and an easel gadget that allows the book to stand up when open, and many other gimmicky bindings.

Because the type of binding is determined by the publisher, it is more practical for writers to categorize cookbooks by content. *General cookbooks*—the good ones are thick and hefty—contain recipes of all kinds, ranging through the menu from appetizers and soups to desserts and beverages, with sections on such topics as canning, freezing, and a host of others. General cookbooks can offer food-related information, such as how to bone a chicken, how to steam vegetables, storage dos and don'ts, nutritive values and/or calorie counts—indeed, almost anything helpful you can think of that has to do with food and cooking.

Category cookbooks are concerned with only one food or one group of foods. The range, obviously, is broad: soups, salads, sauces and dressings, chicken, vegetables, breads, cakes, eggs, pastries, light summer dishes, hearty winter ones, company-coming specialties, and so on. Provided with a sufficiently large market, you could spend a lifetime writing category cookbooks.

Audience-directed cookbooks are put together to serve the needs of a particular group of people: children, teenagers, beginner cooks, accomplished cooks, chefs, caterers, strict vegetarians, lacto-ovo vegetarians, natural-foods buffs, various kinds of medical or weight-loss motivated dieters, and dozens more.

Ethnic cookbooks offer recipes for foods of one kind of people or groups of geographically or religiously linked peoples. For example, one could do an Irish or a Welsh or a Scotch or an English cookbook, or a United Kingdom cookbook bringing together food specialties of all four, or a Commonwealth of Nations cookbook that would add recipes from Canada, Australia, New Zealand, and the smaller islands or countries closely tied to Britain. Range through Europe and you have a dozen subjects to hand—France, Austria, Germany, many more—or through the Middle East or the Far East for extended multiple inspiration. In America, New England, the Deep South, the Midwest, the Far West, all offer possibilities, to say nothing of a state-by-state progression. South of the border, part of this continent and a whole different one offer tempting ideas. Ethnic cookbooks can—and do, and will—go on forever.

Finally, you might wish to classify cookbooks by result: recipes to serve one, to serve two, quantity cookery for those who must feed large groups, budget meals, and so on.

There are two highly specialized categories of cookbooks as well. One is the *commercial cookbook,* prepared for food companies to sell or give away to promote their product(s). Such cookbooks are most often put together by the test-kitchen staff of the food company or of the public-relations firm or advertising agency that services the company, but are sometimes written by an outsider. However, if you are a cookbooking beginner, you are very unlikely—unless, perhaps, you are the niece or nephew of the chairman of the board—to be called on to do a commercial cookbook. Later, if you become well known in the cookbook trade (which doesn't necessarily mean well known to the general public), you may be asked to prepare a commercial cookbook or a series of them. Say yes. It's a struggle all the way, but financially very rewarding.

The second specialized category is what is politely called the *community* (or, less politely, *fund-raiser*) *cookbook.* Community cookbooks can range all the way from lively, attractive, and very useful ones such as those put out by Junior Leagues of cities in various parts of the country to minor efforts so off-putting in appearance and so loaded with errors that both the producers and the buyers would have been better served if the books had never seen the light of day.

Because community cookbooks are considered by almost everyone—the ladies' guild of a church, the docents of a museum, the members of a club, the wives' auxiliary of a symphony orchestra, and dozens of other groups—to be a fun way to raise money, it behooves you to know that if not done properly they can be calamitous budget-busters. And because they are put together by committee—a cumbersome way to accomplish anything—they can be loaded with traps for the unwary. But approached in the right spirit and manned by informed, sensible workers, they can be a pleasure to do and a matter of pride for the sponsoring organization. Almost everything I will have to say in this book applies to community cookbooks as well as to trade and commercial books. But there are special problems, too, that I'll take up later, after we've considered cookbooks in general.

COOKBOOKERY'S WIDE HORIZONS

The business of writing cookbooks is by no means a modern occupation. Consider the Roman general Lucius Licinius Lucullus, who had a few things to say about both war and banquets—his remarks on the latter being considerably more interesting than those on the former—and whose name lives on as an adjective to describe the most sumptuous of edibles. Or remember Epicurus, a Greek of an even earlier time, who may well have been the first atomic physicist but who, because he held that pleasure is the only good and the end of all morality, and espoused the pleasures of the table as one of life's great joys and apparently knew whereof he spoke, is constantly remembered in words derived from his name, epicure and epicurianism.

Those two, and many others who wrote on the subject,

were male, high born, and famous, and that tradition continued for many centuries; even today, many of the most elegant of cookbooks are put together by men, be they professional chefs or gifted amateurs. This tradition seems to have arisen from the twin facts that only the rich and famous could afford the ingredients of a great meal and only they could afford to employ the few inspired fellows who knew how to put those ingredients together into lucullan, epicurean feasts.

In the late eighteenth century, and into the nineteenth, it became obvious that the world was also peopled with more or less ordinary women who labored mightily to put three meals a day on the table for their husbands and children. They needed help, and help was quickly forthcoming from some ladies who knew their way around the kitchen and decided they ought to write a book.

As was the fashion with writers—particularly women writers—of the times, many of these early cookbookers remained anonymous. One took pen in hand in 1830 to prepare *The Frugal Housewife*, "dedicated to those who are not ashamed of economy." As with others of her time, this lady's recipes were imprecise, dotted with measurements such as "a scant cup," "a pinch," "butter the size of a walnut," "a little less than," "as much as can be taken up on the handle of a spoon," and others that would drive a modern cook up the wall. No yields were given and, of course, no cooking temperatures, because there were no stove thermostats. (One of the first cooking instructions I received from my grandmother was to stick my hand into a hot oven and count; if I could reach thirty-five without having to snatch my hand out because I could no longer stand the heat, the oven was "about 350 degrees," just right for a cake. If I could count longer, the oven needed to be "hotted up," or, if a shorter time, the door should be propped open for a couple of minutes to cool it down a bit.)

Another old book, *Cookery Receipts,* by "a leading authority," lumped together cooking directions with home medical advice: Thus, the first three items in her vegetable section concern Celery au Gratin, Spinach on Toast, and Sciatica. Books of this sort often carried advertisements, as well as testimonials from the writer. A bit further along in the vegetable section we have Fried Oyster Plant, Baked Cauliflower, and Stomach Trouble. As to this last, the lady says, "No head is clear for business when there is stomach trouble, and there is no serious stomach trouble after Dr. August Koenig's Hamburg Drops have been taken to cure it."

In the preface to the first edition (1850) of her *The Young Housekeeper's Friend,* Mrs. M. H. Cornelius says:

> I have seen many a young lady, just entering upon the duties of married life, perplexed and prematurely careworn, for want of experience, or a little good instruction, in regard to the simplest domestic processes; and often have felt, with the sincerest sympathy, an earnest wish to render her some effectual aid. If I succeed in affording it through this little book, I shall esteem myself happy; and I have only to ask, in conclusion, that my numerous young friends, and all the youthful housekeepers into whose hands it may fall, will receive it as a token of my friendly interest and best wishes.

As may be seen from this quotation, writing cookbooks is not only a way of earning one's living, but also something of a sacred duty. Thus inspired, go thou and do likewise.

Chapter Two

Getting Organized: Pack-Rat and Bag-Lady Approaches

If you are predisposed to cookbookery, you have probably, like a pack rat—or, if you are a rodent-hater, perhaps being compared to a crow or a magpie makes you more comfortable—been clipping recipes for years and storing them away against a vague "some day." Far-seeing, you may have cut out and kept nonrecipe material concerning food as well, anything from little tidbits of unusual information to whole articles on such subjects as vinegar or tropical fruits or new insights into the nutritional value of sauerkraut or whatever. Practical, you may have tried out a large number of the recipes on your family and friends. Neat, you may have categorized and filed this mass of material; sloppy, you may have hodgepodged it all into a drawer somewhere along with lockless keys, mateless mittens, love letters from someone whose name no longer means anything to you, and unanswered help-wanted ads. Lucky, you may have a legacy of recipes from your mother or grandmother or Great-aunt Jane, who was known far and wide for her salt-rising bread and her steamed puddings. But whatever you've kept and however you've kept it, you do have the necessary jumping-off point for a cookbook.

That, a jumping-off point, is the prime requirement, particularly if you are a first-time-out cookbooker. One day, whether early or late in the save-stuff game, it will dawn on you that you must, absolutely must, do something with this amorphous mass of material you've collected. If you decide to set fire to it and start collecting knitting patterns instead, cookbooks are not your destiny. But if you say to yourself, "Aha! A cookbook!" you're hooked.

For old-pro cookbook writers, it more often works the other way around: You have what seems like a good and unusual cookbook idea first, and start gathering appropriate material for it second. But not always. A few years ago, in the midst of a search for recipes using pâte à chou in ways other than for éclairs and cream puffs, I noted that I had a huge amount of material on cheese. I should, I told myself, propose a cheese cookbook to someone. A few days later I chose an appropriate someone, worked out a proposal, and sent it off. After considerable backing and forthing, in the fullness of time (you will learn that in the cookbook trade time often gets to be pretty darned full), *Cheese Cookery* appeared, enjoyed a comfortable sale, and is still contributing royalty checks to our household income.

So, no matter from whence it comes, your first requirement is a starting place, a jumping-off point, an idea. The second requirement is an enlargement, a refinement, of the first.

THEME AND VARIATIONS

What you need now is a theme, an umbrella under which to shelter a lot of loosely related material and make each piece relevant to all the rest. Your theme will be the answer to the question "What kind of cookbook will this be?" and to find that answer you'll need to ask more questions, such as:

1. *Do I have (or can I produce) recipes for all the various courses of a meal?* If the answer is yes, you have—at least provisionally—the basis of a general cookbook.

2. *Into what category do my best (most unusual, innovative) recipes fall?* The answer to that—entrées, desserts, salads, whatever—indicates the basis of a category cookbook, or perhaps a double-category (soups and salads, for example), or a triple (soups, salads, and sandwiches).

3. *Is there a basic ingredient that occurs more often than any other?* If you have a food that is a particular favorite of yours—chicken, say—or your Aunt Hattie's legacy of recipes leaned heavily in one direction—cheese, perhaps—you may have the basis of a one-food book, augmented for variety's sake by recipes for good go-with foods: dumplings, biscuits, cornbreads, stuffings, and the like for chicken, as an example.

4. *What is the nature of these recipes?* Are they very simple? Everyday recipes well within the capabilities of the average home cook? Quite complicated? Difficult indeed? The answer singles out a possible audience.

5. *What is the origin of the recipes?* Are you a recent arrival? Did Aunt Hattie emigrate from Poland or your mother from Sweden? Do you clip and save information about Greek food because you honeymooned in Greece or South American food because your first love was a Brazilian? You may have the foundations of an ethnic cookbook.

This kind of questing and sorting can go on for hours, and it should—until you have a theme firmly in mind. Then, from the theme, a working title should arise. The working title may be a far cry from the finished title, the one that will eventually appear on the cover or jacket of the book, but it has its own importance. It gives you something by which to call the book —you wouldn't have a child and call it "Hey, you!" for the first few years of its life. Thinking of and speaking of the book by name gives the project substance in your mind and helps to keep you on track, within the bounds of the book's theme. As well, it gives the book a handle by which you and others —family, friends, eventually publishers—can speak of it. The book gains dignity as well as easy recognition if you refer to it as *Cooking Secrets of Hawaii* rather than "that cookbook I'm doing about poi and lomilomi salmon and vegetables steamed in ti leaves and all that other good stuff Hawaiians eat not only at luaus but also in the home."

A ROSE BY ANY OTHER

While we're on the subject, let's pause and take a long, hard look at cookbook titles, both working and finished. First off, a title should be reasonably brief. Long, unwieldy ones foul up the computer, the union catalog, and the publisher's bookkeeping department; even more important, they go in one ear and out the other of a potential purchaser, who then says, "Darn! I can't remember the name of that new cookbook about vegetables. Well, here's one called *Veggies*—that should do fine." (If you are saying to yourself that the shopper could have asked for the book by the author's name, forget it. You might as well face this fact now as later: Unless your name is James Beard or Julia Child, nobody is going to remember it. Ever. Not even if it's Smith.)

Brevity, then, is the first requisite. But wit is not the second; in fact, the reverse is true. Make a heroic effort to restrain yourself from burdening your book with a cutesy title. Keep firmly in mind that, to many people, cutesy equates with insubstantial. One person's cutesy is another's upchuck. Picture to yourself the first reader in a publishing house saying wearily to her friend, the proofreader, "Some bubblehead sent us a cookbook called *Eatsies*, can you imagine?" Forget that your dear firstborn used to call his afternoon snack "wittle wunch." Put out of your mind the fact that your husband, when he feels like a picnic, says, "Let's invite Alf Resco to lunch." Family jokes should be confined to the family; in jokes will be out jokes by the time the book is published. If you can find absolutely nothing to call your book other than *Cookbook,* better that than cute. We have a cat, named Prince Valiant by the grandchildren, who absolutely refuses to answer to anything but "Cat," which proves (I think) that neat is superior to gaudy any day.

A good title should have something to say about the content of the book it graces. *Goodies* connotes small, snack-type, probably sweet foods and is totally inappropriate for a book filled with elegant entrées. *The Best of Boston* would do for a book filled with beans, anadama bread, gooseberry fool, chowders, and the like, or even with colcannon, prawns, and soda bread, but would be a disaster for *canard à l'orange, truite bleu, salade niçoise,* and *soufflé Grand Marnier.* Are you with me? What I'm saying is, use a little good common sense.

In choosing a title, thinking big can lead to trouble. My first hardcover trade cookbook was all about sandwiches, and we hung on it a not-surprising *All About Sandwiches* working title, knowing that we'd change it somewhere along the line. Then the publisher was visited with one of his bolts from the blue. How about *1,000 Fabulous Sandwiches*? Wasn't that a great title? We all agreed that it was, and I went on my way devising new sandwiches and ringing changes on old ones, until one morning I had my own B from the B. What were we thinking of, one thousand sandwiches? The book was to be 244 pages; subtract from that the pages occupied by front matter, by index, by introductions, and I was left with roughly 225 pages to be filled with recipes. At one per page, that would make 225 recipes. At two per page, 450. At three per page—an impossible number, considering the size of the page—675. There was no way, as any fool could plainly see, that we could shoehorn one thousand sandwiches, fabulous or otherwise, into this book. I marched into the publisher's office and pointed this out.

"Nonsense," said he. He was madly in love with that title.

I argued. He argued back. That title was his own, his darling, fruit of his loins, and he wasn't going to give it up without a struggle or even with one.

Finally I told him huffily, "It was you who taught me that a book's title must never lie about its contents."

"Um. Yes." He thought a moment, cleared his throat, and then issued one of those publisher's ukases that make one wish to retreat to one's own office and load one's shotgun. "The title will remain," he said. "It is up to you to devise some way to make the book fit the title."

I went back to my office and sat down to think the problem through. An hour later, I had it. I would go back through the manuscript and add the word *basic* to the title of each of the standard, run-of-the-mill recipes, making them Basic Egg Salad Sandwich, Basic Grilled Cheese, Basic Chicken Sandwich, and so on. Then I would add to each a hefty paragraph of briefly worded variations. For example, for the Basic Egg Salad Sandwich, made with hard-cooked eggs, celery, onion juice, and mayonnaise and served on whole-wheat bread, I suggested adding chopped capers or chopped ripe or green olives or shredded carrot, or chopped green pepper or shredded jícama, or chopped peanuts or walnuts or pecans or salmon caviar, or shredded cheddar or swiss cheese or bits of pimiento or chopped green chilies or cooked leftover vegetables, such as green beans or peas. I suggested seasoning the mayonnaise with lemon juice or prepared mustard or chili sauce or worcestershire or steak sauce, or omitting the mayonnaise and binding the mixture with thousand island dressing or whipped cream cheese or leftover chicken gravy or white sauce. I suggested adding boston lettuce leaves to the sandwich or shredded iceberg lettuce or bean sprouts or alfalfa sprouts or chopped chinese or red cabbage or thin slices of bermuda onion. I suggested substituting for the whole-wheat bread white or rye or cracked wheat or french rolls or kaiser rolls or english muffins or pita.

Are you following this sneaky approach? We now have, depending on how you look at it, either *(a)* one fabulous sandwich with a multitude of variations, or *(b)* thirty-nine fabulous sandwiches, each variation counting as a new creation. How splendid it is to be flexible! The title remained as it was, I didn't have to shoot the publisher after all, and my honor—although perhaps a little bent, a trifle tarnished—emerged virtually unblemished.

Shakespeare and the Bible contribute more than their share when it comes to book titles, but seem to have little to offer, thank goodness, to cookbookers. (As soon as I typed that sentence, *Comfort Me With Apples,* a possible fruit cookbook, leaped into my mind, along with *Loaves and Fishes*—fish and seafood sandwiches—and *Stay Me With Flagons*—cooking with beer, wine, and liquor. And a friend of mine is preparing a book, not concerned with cooking but with a related domestic problem, how to clean anything and everything. Her working title is *Out, Damned Spot!*)

Although it is my firm belief that use of them ought to carry a mandatory prison sentence, puns are beloved of those who pin titles on books. Consider *Wait Reduction Dinners* (quick-and-easy meals), *The Prime of Your Life* (a beef cookbook), to say nothing of *You'll Roux the Day.* Not long ago an acquaintance called to ask what horses eat. Hay, I told her. Plenty of fresh water. A measure of oats night and morning. Sometimes bran mash, made with hot water and a little molasses. For treats, apples, carrots, and the occasional lump of sugar.

"Is that all?" she asked, sounding disappointed.

"That's about it. Horses can't go into a restaurant and order the blue-plate special, you know. Why?"

"Well, I read about that woman who's written a dog-food cookbook, and I thought maybe I could do one for horses."

"Why?" I persisted, growing suspicious.

"I want to call it *Oat Cuisine.*"

Get it? If not, try reading that title out loud.

By now, I have not only made my point but beaten it to death: Titles should be reasonably short, straightforward, clue the reader as to what the book has to offer, and be unfunny or, at worst, only mildly clever.

THE LURE OF LIST-MAKING

I'm big on lists: things to do today, good ideas for birthday presents, foods that are running low, points to make in a lecture on easy but nutritionally sound meals for the elderly. I wouldn't think of going shopping without first making a list of menus for the coming week and from that extrapolating a shopping list. Shopping without a list leads to that budget-buster, impulse buying; besides, you feel like such a fool when you go to make Tuesday night's lemon pie and discover that you forgot to buy lemons.

A list or two or three can be a great help when you've made up your mind to write a cookbook. In fact, lists—the simplest form of outline—comprise the second step in getting started on your book.

Begin by dividing the book into possible sections—chapters, that is, but because "chapter" connotes a certain advancement of the story line, "sections" is a better term for the divisions of a cookbook. If you plan on doing a general cookbook, the sections fall naturally into divisions of a meal. You might have:

- Appetizers
- Soups
- Main dishes (perhaps divided into meat, fish, poultry)
- Salads
- Breads (perhaps divided into quick and yeast)
- Eggs
- Side dishes
- Vegetables and fruit
- Pasta
- Desserts (perhaps divided into cakes and cookies, pies and pastries, puddings and frozen desserts)

And if it is a very large general cookbook, you may want to add sections on cheese, casseroles, canning and preserving, beverages, party foods.

Such a list doesn't mean that you absolutely must have recipes in each of the categories. Nor does it mean you must follow the order of the list, nor that the section titles must be mere flat-footed labels. It means only that you are getting organized, making a beginning. Whether your book is to embrace American cuisine or regional specialties of New England or the Deep South or whatever, or recipes of French or Austro-Hungarian or any other ethnic derivation, or whether they are quick-and-easy or elaborate, the section divisions in the above list will serve you well in helping you to evaluate what you have in hand.

If you are doing a single-topic cookbook, your sections will follow a different pattern, breaking down one of the items on the above list into specifics. Such a breakdown might go like this:

Appetizers: Hors d'oeuvres, canapés, meat appetizers, fish and shellfish appetizers, egg-based, cheese-based, made with puff pastry, made with pâte à chou, dips, spreads, fruit cocktails, shellfish cocktails, appetizer soups, appetizer salads, make-ahead-and-freeze appetizers, little savory sandwiches, homemade breads and crackers—and any other divisions that your recipes may suggest.

Soups: Hot soups, chilled warm-weather soups, ethnic specialties, chowders, main-dish soups, jellied soups, vegetarian soups, meat- and poultry- and fish-based soups, homemade and store-bought soup garnishes, beef and veal and poultry stocks, fish fumé, and others.

Main dishes: Beef, lamb, pork, veal, variety meats, breakfast meats, chicken, game hen, turkey, duck and goose, freshwater fish, saltwater fish, shellfish, egg main dishes, pasta main dishes, cheese main dishes, vegetable main dishes, main-dish salads, meat or fish loaves and pâtés, planned leftovers, main-dish sandwiches, main-dish soups, and others.

Side dishes: White potatoes, yams and sweet potatoes, pasta, gnocchi, cheese, barley, couscous, rice, polenta, wild rice and others, each prepared in many ways.

Vegetables and fruit: Basic vegetable cookery (baking, steaming, frying, deep-frying, boiling, sautéing), stuffed vegetables, creamed vegetables, vegetable combinations, sauces for vegetables, vegetable salads, leftover vegetables; fruit salads, fruit sauces, spiced and/or brandied fruits, compotes, baked compotes, and others (note that here fruits are used only as side dishes, but in a large cookbook, fruit desserts, breads, salads, etc., could be incorporated as well).

Salads: Rundown of salad greens, tossed salads, additions to green salads (such as nuts, croutons, bacon bits, sliced olives, etc.), composed salads, mixed salads, main-dish salads, egg- or cheese-based salads, meat- or poultry- or fish-based salads (using fresh or canned meats and fish), appetizer salads, hot salads, baked salads, and others.

Breads: Yeast loaves (white, rye, whole-wheat, cornmeal, triticale, pumpernickel, sourdough, salt-rising, combinations), Danish rolls (and various fillings), ethnic specialties, quick-bread loaves (banana, cranberry, nut, etc.), casserole breads, batter breads, rolls and buns of all shapes and sizes, coffeecakes, muffins, scones, pancakes, waffles, spoon breads, and more.

Eggs: Basic egg cookery (frying, poaching, scrambling, boiling, hard-cooking, baking, shirring), omelets (both French and puffy), various omelet fillings and inclusions, hard-cooked eggs in various sauces, ethnic egg specialties, egg sandwiches, egg salads, egg main dishes, quiches, custards, sweet and savory soufflés, egg desserts, and others.

Pasta: All the various kinds of pasta and their basic uses, basic cooking methods, flavored pastas, making pasta at home (by hand and by machine), several kinds of red and white lasagnes, sauces for pasta, noodle casseroles and puddings, pasta salads, pasta in soups, and others.

Desserts: Pies and tarts (and all the various pastries used for them), puff pastry and its uses, pâte à chou and its uses, various kinds of meringues and their uses, foam cakes, chiffon cakes, butter cakes, fruit cakes, cupcakes and petits fours, filled and rolled cakes, cake frostings and fillings, soufflés and related desserts, puddings (stovetop, baked, steamed), cookies (rolled, drop, bar, refrigerator), bavarians and other gelatin desserts, fruit desserts, ice creams, sherbets, other frozen desserts, and more.

If you wish to add other recipe sections to any book, follow this same cover-all-the-bases system in plotting your working strategy.

ENTER THE BAG LADY

There are all sorts of systems for keeping track of the materials you have and for bringing at least a semblance of order to a large amount of material that may very well consist of handfuls of clippings and a bunch of file cards and/or slips of paper with notes scribbled on them. The simplest—but also, unfortunately, the least useful—is an A-through-Z file, which divides your masses of material into twenty-six smaller masses but isn't a great deal of help in finding what you're looking for quickly and easily. A file, divided by meals, with separate accommodation in each division for each of the food categories on our by-meal list, will enable you to locate items more readily. And if—as I do, after years of writing cookbooks and as many years of industrious clipping and note-making and saving—you have a very large amount of material to deal with, a by-category file broken into separate foods, combined with a by-meal cross-reference file organized in the A-through-Z method, serves very well indeed.

I worked out this system when I was preparing to write the bulkiest book I've ever tackled: 624 pages, containing in the neighborhood of a million words. On top of a counter-height row of cabinets, my husband built a sort of trough for me, about eight feet long and just wide enough to comfortably accommodate legal-size file folders; the whole thing was surrounded by a six-inch retaining wall and spaced with high-standing dividers lettered A through Z. Behind each divider, I placed a file, appropriately labeled, for each food or meal component or basic ingredient, plus a general letter file to harbor small scraps of one-of-a-kind information.

To give you a better idea, my A file contained:

A (general information)
A LA
ABALONE
ABBREVIATIONS IN RECIPES
ACIDOPHILUS
ACIDS
ACORN SQUASH
ADDITIVES AND PRESERVATIVES
ADULTERANTS
AGNEAU
AKEES
AL DENTE
ALBACORE
ALBONDIGAS
ALE
ALESSANDRI
ALFALFA SPROUTS
ALKALIS
ALLERGIES, FOOD
ALLIGATOR PEARS
ALL-PURPOSE FLOUR
ALLSPICE
ALMOND EXTRACT
ALMOND PASTE
ALMONDS
ALPINO
ALUMINUM FOIL
ALUMINUM POTS, PANS, KITCHEN UTENSILS
AMANDINE
AMINO ACIDS
AMORINI
ANCHOVIES
ANGEL FOOD CAKES
ANISE
ANTELOPE
ANTIOXIDANTS
ANTIPASTO
APÉRITIFS
APHRODISIAC FOODS
APPETIZERS

APPLE-PIE SPICE
APPLES
APPLIANCES
APRICOTS
ARABIC BREADS
ARLES
ARROWROOT
ARTICHOKES, GLOBE
ARTICHOKES, JERUSALEM
ARTIFICIAL FLAVORS
ARTIFICIAL SWEETENERS
ASIAGO
ASPARAGUS
ASPIC
AU GRATIN
AU JUS
AU LAIT
AUBERGINE
AVGOLEMONO
AVOCADOS

Whew! And whew! again, when you consider that this is only one letter of the alphabet, with twenty-five more to go. Intimidating, I admit. But I'd rather be intimidated than frustrated any day, and with this file I am never frustrated because I can find anything I need, *anything,* in no time flat. I've added to the file since I began it, of course—added both new entries and additional items in old categories. Now, when I sit down at my typewriter to work on anything to do with food, this master file is only a step away. To my right is a small bookcase holding general and food-related reference books. Just beyond, shelf after shelf of cookbooks. All this comes as a continuing marvel to my family and friends, because I am not by nature particularly neat. I simply point out, with a smug smile, that there is a great deal of difference between being neat and being organized, and go on typing.

Why "bag lady," you ask? Because all this wealth of information is contained in legal-size file bags, or envelopes, not file folders. They are made of the same material (tag stock, to be technical) as file folders, but are far superior because they have closed sides. A file folder filled with odd-shaped and odd-sized materials will strew some of its contents behind if it is carried around, like Hansel and Gretel leaving a trail of crumbs. But the file bag, closed on three sides, keeps its contents securely within. File bags cost slightly more than folders, but they're worth it. Choose legal size, which will accommodate almost anything you want to file.

WHERE DO ALL THOSE RECIPES COME FROM?

It goes without saying that you can't do a cookbook without recipes. So why am I saying it? Because the world is filled with people who, equipped with a file of twenty-three recipes (four of them duplicates) and a monstrous ego, embark blithely on cookbooking without thinking twice. Twice? Once. Some of them fall by the wayside, but many persevere. Where do these, the ones who manage to write cookbooks without being in any way prepared to do so, get their recipes? Why, they steal them, of course.

This is not to say that every recipe in every cookbook published should be brand new, bearing no resemblance to any recipe in any cookbook previously published. Just as there is nothing new under the sun, there is nothing new in the kitchen. Nothing *totally* new, that is. But new ingredients appear on the market, and we learn to use them. New techniques are developed, and we embrace them. New appliances are invented, and we love (or hate) them. New styles of cooking, new insights on food come to the fore, and we take them to our hearts. A cookbook published today will bear little resemblance to one published twenty, thirty, forty, fifty years ago unless the resemblance is intentional, if the book is meant to be nostalgic in nature. Even then the recipes will have been updated to conform with modern kitchens and their contents.

In colonial times, for example, flour was always damp and had to be dried out in front of the fire before it could be used. Sugar came in a pressed cone covered with blue paper, and had to be shaved off the cone before it could be measured. But no colonial-style cookbook published today, no matter how nostalgic, is going to direct the home cook to dry out the flour and shave the sugar before proceeding with the recipe. In a cookbook published as short a time as ten years ago, there would have been no recipe for the kiwi tart that is so dear to the hearts of today's cookbookers, simply because there were no fuzzy, egg-shaped little kiwifruit in the markets. Ditto macadamia nuts, and a dozen more "new" ingredients. No cookbook of thirty years ago would have told the home cook how to make a chiffon cake, because the method had not yet been devised. And if you did make a cake from that cookbook, you'd be told to flavor it with vanilla extract, or possibly lemon extract, or barely possibly almond extract, but today you'd have your choice of in the neighborhood of forty-five available flavoring extracts, ranging from the familiar through the exotic to the gee-whiz-why-did-they-do-this.

So there are, indeed, new things in the kitchen. Food, like love, is at once constant and ever changing. Unfortunately, some of the new things are fads, and as a cookbooker you'll have to learn to spot and avoid them, lest in the nine-month gestation period of a book the fad disappears and there you are, with *oeufs en gelée* on your face. Trifle for dessert appears to have run its course. Sushi, on the other hand, seems to have spread its charms to other sorts of raw-fish dishes, from ceviche to gravad lax, although it's unlikely—because of the relatively small number of people who truly like both the food and the idea of it, as well as the relatively small number of ways to prepare it, plus the fact that many kinds of raw fish harbor flukes that can cause disastrous stomach and intestinal problems—that single-subject raw-fish cookbooks will suddenly begin to appear. Pasta seems to be coming to the end of its fad period; however, because it is so good, can be prepared so many ways, and is relatively inexpensive, pasta will continue to have its place in many cookbooks. Chocolate is, and doubtless will always be, the delight of lovers of sweets, but it is doubtful that there will be too many more all-chocolate cookbooks, simply because everything that there is to say about chocolate has already been said ten times over. Beef Wellington, although it is delicious and is still often served, has not been *de rigueur* at elegant dinner parties for some time; on the other hand, Pocketbook Steak (sirloin stuffed with oysters), which a number of my trendy friends assured me would take the place of Beef Wellington, never did put in an appearance.

Food fads come and go. Some stay quite a while, some fade away almost at once. Some disappear from fad status but find themselves a welcome place in everyday menus. Some foods —chicken is an example—have always been very popular and always will be. When you set out to do a cookbook, particularly a first cookbook, by all means include recipes (if they're suitable to your theme) for truly good fad dishes, but don't fall into the trap of doing an all-fad-food book, which may well be out of date before you've typed the last word of the manuscript.

A LICENSE TO STEAL?

A recipe cannot be copyrighted—everyone in the cookbook business "knows" that. Like a great many other statements of what people believe to be fact, that one is true, but not quite. True: A recipe's ingredients and the order in which they are listed and used cannot be copyrighted. Also true: All the remaining elements of a cookbook can be and usually are copyrighted—the wording of the recipe comment, the wording of the recipe method, the general and the section introductions, the wording of captions for illustrations as well as the illustrations themselves. In other words, a fact cannot be copyrighted, but the manner of presenting that fact can be. So if there is larceny in your heart, watch yourself.

Even if the idea of larceny isn't disturbing, common sense ought to tell you that lifting intact whole batches of recipes from someone else's published cookbook is not only a scurvy trick, but a silly one. Other people in this world read—and remember—cookbooks and food articles in magazines and newspapers. If you claim someone else's efforts as your own, someone else's ideas as yours, someone else's inventions as original with you, sooner or later you'll be caught. You won't be flogged or locked up in a dungeon, but no publisher will put out the books you offer, and no readers, if the books do get into print, will buy them.

This is not to say that recipes aren't stolen right and left. The name of the recipe is changed, and some small alteration is made in the recipe itself, such as substituting mace for nutmeg, garnishing with watercress instead of parsley, using mashed sweet potatoes instead of squash. A good deal of the time, nobody notices. Even more of the time, nobody complains, particularly if the recipe was no great shakes in the first place.

Many years ago, long before the cool-rise method of raising yeast breads was common practice, I worked out a recipe for rich, delicate sweet rolls, made with ample butter and sour cream but no sugar and set to rise overnight in the refrigerator; next day they were treated to the roll-and-turn method, as in puff pastry, although layered not with butter but with vanilla sugar scented with a bit of nutmeg. They were unusual and delicious. I promptly incorporated them in my next cookbook, and thought nothing more about it—until, a year or so later, some woman won a national bake-off with the identical recipe. I wrote the woman a letter I hope blistered her eyeballs in the reading, but other than that there was little I could do. Sue? Hardly. I've had a lot of recipes lifted from my cookbooks since, but none that galled me as much as that one.

There are a great many sources—legitimate sources—to use as you gather material for your cookbook. These are the most common, and most useful:

1. *Standard recipes.* There are dozens, even hundreds, of these, a number of which appear in almost every cookbook that comes on the market. As an example, consider pastry for pies and tarts. There are only so many such pastries—pâte brisée, pâte sucrée, cream-cheese pastry, flour-paste pie dough, hot-water crust, no-roll crust, oil pie dough, and mürbeteig are the most familiar ones—and even the additions to them, such as shredded cheese or spices or ground nuts, have become standards. The same is true of other pastries, such as pâte à pâté, flaky pastry (quick puff paste), pâte feuilletée, Danish pastry, pâte à chou, meringue paste, phyllo (filo), and strudel dough. All have become so standardized that a recipe

for any or several can appear, in exactly the same form, in any number of cookbooks.

2. *Legacy recipes.* These are the handed-down pleasures of the table that have come to you from family sources, and that are often very good and unusual. Just bear in mind that such recipes must be updated to take into consideration present-day ingredients and cooking methods, and that old doesn't always mean good—make certain to test them, not once but several times, to be sure that the results are as delicious as you remember them and the method foolproof.

3. *Your innovations and experiments.* You may say on first blush that you've never invented a single recipe, but if you're a good cook that probably isn't true. Your way with so common a dish as pot roast may well be different from anyone else's, and as for your caramel torte—well, as guests assure you, there's never been anything half so good. Innovations and experiments of your family and friends are also fair game, but again, be sure to test them. In this category, too, go recipes given you by chefs and other professional cooks. Again, test carefully, with particular regard to quantities of ingredients. Chefs work from memory and are notoriously vague when asked to commit their specialties to paper, especially to serve fewer than fifty people.

4. *Adapted recipes.* Although it is not considered cricket to use another professional food writer's originations published in cookbooks and magazine or newspaper articles, there is no stigma attached to adapting them—that is, making substantial, not merely inconsequential,

changes in the recipes. Just bear firmly in mind that "adapt" and "adopt" are not synonymous, and make sure to test several times to be certain that your first inspiration wasn't just a lucky fluke.

5. *Recipes from old cookbooks.* There are a great many good dishes hiding in the pages of out-of-date cookbooks. These forgotten or overlooked books can be a treasure-house of delightful recipes. Update them, test them, and use them with pleasure. Where do you find such recipes? In the books your mother and grandmother used, if they are still around. In cookbooks picked up at rummage sales and flea markets. In the library. From the catalogs of houses that specialize in these books, such as Grove Press and Dover, and bookstores that sell cookbooks exclusively, such as Jessica's Biscuit (see page 247).

6. *Frankly swiped recipes.* If for some reason—and it should be a good one—you wish to use a recipe from another food professional, you can do so without guilt if you give credit where it is due. Say something like this: "No Greek-style party would be complete without moussaka, and I believe that Craig Claiborne's recipe is one on which it's not possible to improve, so here it is."

7. *Food-association recipes.* No matter what you eat, you can be reasonably certain that there is a food association somewhere backing up every mouthful—organizations such as the Idaho Potato Board, the Avocado Advisory Council, the Washington and Idaho Pea and Lentil Commission, the National Livestock and Meat Board, the California Beef Council, the Cling Peach Advisory

Board, and dozens more. Write to any of these, tell them what you are doing and what you need, and they'll be happy to help. Find their addresses in any of several directories of associations to which a librarian will be glad to point the way.

8. *Food manufacturers' and packagers' recipes.* From one end of the country to the other, there are convocations of females (there are virtually no men—yet—in this field) who work for companies that put out food products, or for the advertising agencies or public-relations firms that are hired by those companies. Their profession is home economist, their workplace a test kitchen—usually cheerfully decorated and equipped with every imaginable convenience—and their mission is to create and test recipes that incorporate generous amounts of their employer's products. These are the recipes that appear on the labels of cans and packages or on small brochures attached to them, in leaflets that the companies mail out in answer to requests, in cookbooks that the companies give away or sell at or below cost, in advertisements in magazines and newspapers and on radio and television. Because the aim of all this work that results in all these recipes is to Spread the Word concerning the company's products, the recipes usually are not protected in any way and are generally available for the taking.

However, as with almost anything that comes for free, there is a caveat attached to recipes from both food associations and food companies and, indeed, to any recipe that you haven't trumped up from scratch in your own kitchen. Test it! Don't tell yourself that because the recipe came from what journalists call a "reliable source" it must be good. There is no guarantee, because what is one person's treat is often another's garbage. Besides, those good ladies in the test kitchen develop blind spots where their company's products are concerned, and can talk themselves into believing that sauerkraut with chocolate sauce is a yummy inspiration. And when the company is pressing for just one more recipe, or just ten, or just a hundred, there are bound to be some real bummers in the lot.

One of the truly horrid memories of an otherwise happy childhood concerns the day my mother tried a recipe gleaned from an ad in the now-defunct *Woman's Home Companion.* She took a big, thick, juicy sirloin steak, seared it on each side, covered it with sliced bananas (the recipe title was Tropical Smothered Steak, which you'd think would have warned her away at the start), sprinkled the bananas with cinnamon, and baked the whole thing until it screamed for mercy. I have no words to describe the way it looked when finally taken from the oven, although "pre-eaten" may give you a clue, and I'll spare you the comments of my father, the gourmet.

So test, and if you're not sure, test again, before you include any recipe, from whatever source, in a cookbook that will carry your name and reputation.

TECHNIQUES OF RECIPE TESTING

You've doubtless seen the phrases "home tested" and "kitchen tested" in reference to recipes and cookbooks. "Home tested" means that the recipes have been tested in somebody's—or several somebodies'—home, by a home cook, in a kitchen with the usual home-type stove and refrigerator and other appliances. "Kitchen tested" tells you that the recipes were tested in the kitchens of the company or the magazine or newspaper offering them, or in special commercial kitchens that do nothing except test recipes sent to them by food companies or by magazines or newspapers. Such kitchens are generally equipped with latest-model refrigerators and freezers, both gas and electric stoves, all the newest and best appliances and gadgets. If something gets out of whack, it is repaired at once. Ovens are calibrated regularly to make certain that the temperature they show is the temperature they deliver. Not least of the joys of a test kitchen is the herd of scullions who peel and chop and mince and dice, who wash the dishes as fast as they are dirtied, who whisk away the garbage as soon as it's created, who constantly clean up after you. Combine all this service with the fact that the people in charge are professionals, experts, and it's no wonder that kitchen-tested triumphs once in a while turn out to be home-tested disasters. No home kitchens, no home cooks, can expect to measure up. (Anyway, don't believe for a moment that the experts never make mistakes. They do, and those mistakes can be real lulus.)

So don't downgrade yourself, dig your toe in the dirt, and mutter that these recipes of yours "haven't been tested anywhere but in my own kitchen." Your own kitchen is just the same as, or marginally better or marginally worse than, the kitchens in which home cooks using your cookbook will prepare your recipes. If they are successful in your kitchen, they will be successful in other home kitchens, as long as you bear in mind these five basic cautions.

1. *Don't call for ingredients that are not readily available throughout the country.* The exception is in elegant or ethnic

cookbooks, whose users can be assumed to be willing to mail-order ingredients not found locally; even so, make sure to give readers names and addresses of mail-order sources.

2. *Don't call for very expensive ingredients,* such as imported caviar, truffles, and the like, unless your cookbook is aimed at an audience to whom, presumably, money is no object.

3. *Don't call for the use of appliances or gadgets that the average home cook cannot be reasonably expected to have in his or her kitchen.* For example, all kitchens have knives, most have electric mixers, many have blenders, and about half have food processors. Use phrases that offer an alternative, such as "with a knife or in a food processor," or "in blender or food processor." Many recipes still offer an alternative to the electric mixer, as "beat 2 minutes at medium speed, or 150 strokes by hand," but that is no longer really necessary.

4. *Keep up with the times.* Today's recipes cut down on or omit salt and often call for unsalted butter, which until a short time ago was hard to come by in some areas but is now widely available. When appropriate, cut animal fats to a minimum, or substitute polyunsaturated fats. Except in elegant cookbooks, where butter is likely to be a must in many recipes, call for "butter or margarine" rather than butter only.

5. *If a recipe will produce what may be, to the average cook, an unexpected result, point this out in a note or comment.* "Batter will be very thin," for example.

PAPERWORK IN THE KITCHEN

The use of *test sheets* when you test recipes is an orderly, trouble-saving habit. True, you can scribble your recipes on odd pieces of paper, make notes all over the margins, dribble them with samples of whatever you're cooking, and generally, at the close of a testing session, end up with a gloppy mess that looks as if it were the site the cat chose to have her kittens, but you'll rue the day. Test sheets make safer and easier the task of typing recipes for the manuscript—better for you, absolutely necessary if someone else is to do the typing. Test sheets become file copies of the recipes used in each book, filed two-by-two with copies of the recipes as they were sent to the publisher, so they can be located easily and referred to quickly if something goes wrong or gets lost. And if an editor or a home ec at a food company says, "I'd like to see your test sheets on these," you can produce them with a flourish instead of hastily describing to him or her how cute the kittens were.

Test sheets can't be found in stationery stores, but producing them is a simple cottage industry. See the sample sheet on the next page, change it or add to it so it is most useful to you, and then have it photocopied, preferably on some bright-colored paper quite different from the white you use for manuscripts. Fill in the preliminaries—code, ingredients, method—place the sheets to be used at the particular testing session on a clipboard, have a pen or pencil handy for making notes and filling in blanks, and you're in business. If you get into a jam with a particularly recalcitrant recipe and run out of space, start a fresh test sheet for it, but staple the old one to the back so you'll have it for reference.

TEST SHEET

Recipe title_____________________ Recipe #_____

For__________________ Section________________

Date tested_______ Test #_____ Weather_________

- -

PREP TIME____________ COOK TIME__________

PAN(S)________________ PAN PREP____________

COOKING TEMP_______ STORAGE___________

INGREDIENTS:

METHOD:

COMMENTS:

CONCLUSION:

YOU CAN'T WORK WITHOUT TOOLS

A cookbooker's kitchen should be convenient, cheerful, and well equipped. You need plenty of cupboard and counter space and larger amounts as well as a larger variety of ingredients than the average kitchen boasts. Appliances need not be brand new, but should be up to date and kept in first-class condition. A good, reliable stove is a necessity, as is a modern refrigerator—preferably one larger than the usual family requires. You can conceivably get along without a separate freezer, but if you do, you'll be wasting a great deal of perfectly good food that could otherwise be stored for later use, whether by you or by someone else. A dishwasher is a must, and so is getting into the habit of using it practically, placing dishes and pots in it as soon as they are used, turning it on as soon as it is full.

You'll need small appliances, too, most likely in larger numbers than the average kitchen boasts, because you will want to direct your readers in the use of many of them, at least as alternatives to more basic methods in recipes. Certainly a microwave oven would seem to be a necessity today. A convection oven is not absolutely necessary, but very useful. Electrical appliances such as skillet, slow cooker, and deep fryer are a big help in determining exact cooking temperatures to tell your readers. An electric slicer is very useful, but as most kitchens don't have them, you can't direct readers to their use, except in the event that you are doing a small-appliance cookbook. You must have an electric mixer and a blender; a food processor is a necessity, too, so that readers can at least be directed to its use as an alternative.

"Pay attention to small things and the big ones will take

care of themselves" is a bare-faced lie, but the first part of that saying is good advice. Knives must be sharp, and in wide variety. Everything in your kitchen must be in tip-top shape, repaired immediately when necessary, replaced when overcome by age. Stock your kitchen so you'll never have to search out a substitute for a needed tool.

On the other hand, don't fall so deeply in love with any of your equipment that you use it unwisely—and worse, call for its unwise use in your recipes. If you need a tablespoon of minced onion, don't use, and then have to wash, the food processor; to cope with so small an amount sensibly, think back to the day when a knife and a cutting board were your mincing tools. And remember that all tools are not created equal: Your food processor may grind coffee beans well, but some brands won't; some (few) blenders grind nuts reasonably well, but more produce an oily mess; some electric knife sharpeners do a good job, others decorate the blades with nicks and scratches.

If you are the kind of cook who buys every nutsy gadget that comes on the market, fine. Go ahead and enjoy your toys. But don't call for their use in a cookbook, because most of the cooks out there don't know the gadgets exist or, if they do, either can't afford them or wouldn't be caught dead with them.

As you become known in the cookbook business, manufacturers will often send you their latest inventions, hoping that you'll use and enjoy them, and hoping even more that you'll mention them in your cookbooks. I have three such right now. One is an electrically plugged-in holder that supports four tools—a whisk, a scraper, a spatula, and a device for stirring. The container constantly recharges the tools, so they can be plucked out and carried to stove or counter for use without the inconvenience of an electric cord trailed behind. I use it often and I like it, particularly at times when my arthritis is kicking up. The second is an electric sauce maker, into which one puts the ingredients for a sauce or a pudding or other mixture that requires constant low temperature and what can seem like years of stirring. Plug in the appliance and it cooks gently, obligingly stirring the mixture all the while until it is done, while one goes about one's business elsewhere. It does its job well, but prodded by the Work Ethic under which I was brought up, I tend to feel rather guilty at not doing my own stirring. The third is an object, shaped rather like a plump guided missile, that purports to do everything but brush teeth and shine shoes. After it has measured, chopped, mixed, or whatever, it turns itself on and cooks what's inside. Its retail price is about equal to the cost of an arm and a leg, and I am somewhat suspicious of it—anything so efficient, so time-saving, must have an ulterior motive.

My wariness about breakthroughs in the kitchen stems from microwave ovens. Many years ago, before the ovens were put on the market, a friend and I were hired to do the first microwave oven cookbook, to be packed with the first ovens presented to a waiting world. In due course the things arrived—nineteen of them, for heaven's sake—accompanied by a document, translated literally from the Japanese, long on politesse and short on technicalities. I stared at the ovens for a couple of hours, and then invited an engineer friend to dinner. He was able to figure out the fine points for me, and to discover that the manufacturer knew what he was doing when he shipped us nineteen ovens: Twelve did not work at all, and two worked only part-time.

I still recall the surge of joy we felt when something turned out right—crispy bacon, dry and fluffy rice, chocolate melted but not burned. I also remember the problems—cakes with what seemed to be a layer of mucilage on top, chicken drumsticks overcooked halfway down but raw from that point on, roasts that were dishwater-colored and tasted boiled, the morning that I baked thirty-four cup custards, one at a time, before any turned out to my satisfaction. Finally, working on the try-try-again principle, we finished the wretched book. As we packed up the ovens to return them, I remarked to my friend, "These things will never catch on." Vehemently, she agreed with me.

TAKE OFF YOUR APRON!

Now that you've decided to venture into cookbookery, you'll need the tools of a second trade: equipment for writing and a place in which to write.

However appropriate it may seem at first, the end of that kitchen table is *not* a good place to set up your cookbook office. Aside from the fact that a little dribbled applesauce or a dropped egg can play hob with a typewriter's innards, you'll now be spending more time than ever before in the kitchen and will need a place of refuge from it. What with all the testing—and retesting and re-retesting—of recipes, you'll feel sufficiently put-upon without having to do your writing in the same environment. A corner of living room or bedroom or family room or even the laundry room will do, but if you possibly can, set aside a room, no matter how small, to be your office and only your office, where nothing but writing is ever done.

Why? Because you'll feel much more efficient, much more professional, with an office of your own, one in which your equipment can live permanently instead of having to be set up before you can start each session, put away after you are through. Also, you'll be interrupted less often if you can go into your office and shut the door behind you than if you're somewhere out in the open. And there is considerable tax advantage—ask your lawyer or accountant—to having a room that is used only as a place in which to write.

What will you need by way of equipment? A typewriter, certainly; even if you are a wretched typist, your first drafts should be typed, and there are always letters to write and letters to be answered. All the normal run of supplies: typing paper, pens and pencils, carbon paper, scratch pads, file cards, clips, tape—the works. If you don't have a business letterhead, now is the time to have one designed and printed. Not surprisingly, business letters appear much more businesslike typed on a professional letterhead than written on the pale pink paper you use for correspondence with Aunt Ella. Reference books—you'll find some appropriate ones listed on pages 242–243—should be shelved nearby, and so should your library of cookbooks. Filing cabinets or other holders for your files should be easily accessible. A typewriter stand, a desk or table at which you can read and edit manuscripts, and a comfortable but supportive chair, plus good light by which to work, are necessities. If at all possible, have a telephone extension on your desk, so you won't have to go flying a dozen times an hour to answer a phone ringing in another room. And even though the very idea reduces you to a cold sweat, you will have to learn to keep books. Get a ledger or a notebook—anything that you reserve solely for the one purpose—and record (each entry dated) both income and disbursements, the latter including tools and equipment you purchase for each project, and the cost of food used in testing recipes. Not exactly fun, but not exactly an unbearable burden.

So you're ready to go to work. Is work ready for you? Have you made (and, if necessary, revised) an outline? Are your files for this book segregated from your general files, and reordered to conform with the outline? Have you a pile of tested recipes beside you? Then have at it!

COPING WITH A COOKBOOK'S BY-PRODUCTS

Shortly after you start testing recipes, you will be stunned by the amazing, not to say appalling, amount of food this activity generates. Failures, of course, can be thrown out without a qualm. But it takes a strong heart and a cold conscience to tip successes into the garbage can, particularly if you have been raised by a mother who enticed you to clean your plate at every meal with tales of starving children the world over.

What on earth do you do with all that food? Have it for dinner. Freeze it for another day. Store up goodies in your freezer until you have enough to throw a big party. Be a good neighbor and share up and down the street. Call friends and family to say that you have their dinner entrée waiting if they care to pick it up. Stockpile in the freezer against the church supper or covered-dish dinner or whatever that's upcoming. Donate food to a children's home or a shelter for battered wives or a mission or a halfway house that will welcome your support. Become a volunteer hospital or prison visitor and go armed with treats. Pack up nonperishables and ship them off to your kids at college. If you work up a team of recipe testers, as you will probably want to do once you're well into cookbooking, the problem will be at least partially solved: Them as tests eats. (Speaking of testers, I have two stepdaughters, one goddaughter, three sisters-in-law, and several friends and neighbors who can be called on to rally round at testing time, and you should be able to develop a like support team to help you; just make certain that the ones you choose aren't kitchen klutzes. There are also women in every town of any size, usually retired home economists, who will home-test recipes for a fee; the trick is to dig them out, but sooner or later if you're working on a cookbook they'll surface, having learned of you through some grapevine or other.)

Comfort yourself with this: Before the days of home freezers, the problem of what to do with tested food was considerably more knotty. At one point in that long-gone time, I contracted to do a cookie cookbook. The idea pleased me, but the thought of all those cookies made me slightly ill before I even began to test. Then inspiration struck. I went up and down the street, talking neighbors into a plan. Each of us would devote a full day, shortly before Christmas, to making cookies according to recipes I would supply, and we would donate the cookies to the local Shriners' Hospital for Crippled Children. It worked out very well. Thirty-four of us made literally thousands and thousands of cookies. Our hearts were warmed. The children were delighted. It was a beautiful project.

Cookbooking, as you will learn, has its rewards—financial, gastronomical, and once in a while even spiritual.

Chapter Three

Show and Tell: The Fine Art of Writing Recipes

This is the point at which neatness truly counts: neatness in the recipe on the page, and neatness in the attitude of the writer who puts it there. Keep your wits about you, because mistakes are disastrous, loose ends anathema, omissions calamitous. Likewise, no matter how proud you are of it, how prone to show it off, save your extensive vocabulary for other occasions. Say what you have to say as simply and clearly as possible, deny yourself the pleasure of using five words where one will do the job, then shut up and go on to the next recipe.

All that is by no means meant to imply that a once-over-lightly treatment is sufficient. Recipe writing, as does every kind of writing, requires thought. Even when you've become an old hand at the game, recipe writing is not a matter simply of rolling a piece of paper into the typewriter and firing away, because each recipe is different from every other. If you don't—or can't—make those differences clear, you're not doing what you set out to do. Mistakes in a recipe are unpardonable—but unfortunately easy to make, and often made. And generally, they are sins of omission.

Say that you're trying out a new cake recipe. If you are a methodical cook, you will have assembled all the ingredients and made them ready for use—measured the milk, combined the dry ingredients, and so on. You will have followed the instructions concerning preparing the pan and preheating the oven. Now you're ready to go. Following directions in the method, you beat the eggs until whites and yolks are well blended, then beat in the sugar. The next instruction is: "Slowly add butter, continuing to beat." Ah, the butter. *What* butter? You have none laid out. A hasty review of the list of ingredients offers no help; there is no mention of butter. Another look at the mixture in the bowl tells you that if you add solid butter to it, even cut into small pieces and even adding it while you continue to beat, you'll get a suspension (a series of small particles distributed throughout) rather than an emulsion (a combination of all ingredients into a homogeneous whole). You look at the method again, and decide that the key word is "slowly." It is difficult, if not impossible, to add solid butter slowly; even if the butter is cut up, the instruction should be to add "a little at a time" or, better, "one piece at a time" as you continue to beat. But melted butter can be added slowly, in a thin stream. Good. You decide to melt the butter. All right, but how much butter? At that point, you may—while calling down assorted curses on the head of the thumb-fingered dolt who wrote the book—decide to abandon the whole project, or you may make a guess at the amount, forge ahead, and see what eventuates. If you are a good cook, a practiced cook, a cook who knows a bit about food chemistry, you'll often be able to fight your way through messes like this one and come out smiling. But how about the beginning cook, who barely knows what he or she is doing when the recipe is in perfect shape?

A second common recipe writing mistake is the "Oops, unexpected leftovers!" syndrome. Moving happily about your kitchen, humming under your breath, you follow a new recipe's instructions to mince sufficient mushrooms to make 1 cup and to melt 2 tablespoons of butter in a skillet over medium heat. Next: "Sauté mushrooms in butter until liquid has evaporated and they just begin to brown. Remove from heat and set aside." You do so, and then follow the recipe's instructions for the remainder of the ingredients: poaching chicken and using the broth to make béchamel; steaming, draining, and chopping spinach; cooking fettuccine. Keeping an eye on the recipe, you layer fettuccine, then spinach, then chicken, then béchamel in a casserole, and repeat. Finally you top the dish with a mixture of buttered fresh bread crumbs, snipped parsley, and freshly grated romano, salivating delicately as you anticipate how good it is going to taste.

You are about to pop it in the oven when the mushrooms, skulking unused in their skillet, catch your eye. You run back through the recipe. After being sautéed and set aside, they are never mentioned again. Where were they to be used? As a separate layer? Perhaps mixed with the spinach, which turned out to be a bit skimpy? Well, no matter. Such questions are now academic, as the casserole is finished and its topping in place. You put the casserole in the oven, refrigerate the mushrooms to use in soup for tomorrow's lunch, and go about your business, vowing never to trust that particular cookbook again.

A third problem is the throw-away, or "trash-too-soon," syndrome. The recipe instructs you to use a 7-ounce can of tuna, drained. Later it tells you to combine vinegar and garlic with the oil drained from the tuna. But without the instruction to reserve the tuna oil, five will get you ten that you threw it away when you got the tuna ready to use. Chalk another one up to experience.

So—the cardinal rule of recipe writing: Make absolutely certain that all ingredients appear in the ingredients list, and that all of them are properly used in the method.

There are certain absolutes for every recipe, essential elements that must appear.

Title

The title need not state flat-footedly what the recipe is about, but it should give a clue. "Scalloped Turnips" is admittedly dull, but it is superior to "Mama's Favorite," which doesn't tell the reader a thing. Compromise on "Mama's Spicy Turnip Scallop," which, if not exactly sparkling, is at least serviceable. Steer clear of foreign titles unless the cookbook is to be an elegant one or a collection of ethnic recipes, or unless the words are so familiar they have become common usage; certain foreign-language words—soufflé, guacamole, scaloppini (or scallopini), and dozens more—have become so common that they are now a part of English. This is true, too, of such phrases as "à la mode" and "al dente." These terms are acceptable in recipe titles. But if there's any doubt, translate. "Tripes à la Mode de Caen" is iffy in a nuts-and-bolts cookbook—better make it "Tripe Caen Style"—but perfectly acceptable in an elegant cookbook.

Whatever the language, stay away from mixed-bag titles in which words of two languages mingle uncomfortably. Make it "Suprêmes de Volaille" or "Breast of Chicken," but never, never "Chicken Suprêmes." In all cases, make sure necessary diacritical marks are correct and correctly in place. (Exception: Titles written entirely in capital letters carry no diacritical marks when the book is in English; in another language—Spanish is one—they may.)

Yield

The number of servings that may be expected from the dish is called the "yield." This figure should appear on the same line as the title, just below the title, or at the end of the recipe. Obviously, a dish served to a bunch of stevedores will not yield as many servings as the same one served to a gaggle of ladies on diets, but in offering yields you're supposed to consider the average family, consisting of two adults and two children—culinary arts do not take into account that one-half child sociological treatises are constantly citing. Again, the food's position in the meal should be taken into consideration; pasta served as an appetizer will yield more portions than when the same quantity is offered as a main dish. More servings can be expected from a dish served at a buffet, where there are many other choices, than at a sit-down dinner, where the entrée is the entrée, take it or leave it. Keep that family of four in mind, and you'll be on solid ground.

Convention once said that yield should be expressed as "serves 4"—or 6 or 8, or whatever. Now we approach it the other way, with "4 servings," and there is a good reason. "Serves 4" means that each of four people can have a helping of this dish, but "4 servings" indicates how many ordinary, average servings the dish supplies, so that if you are feeding a teenage boy—or worse, two or three—or Aunt Hessie who eats like a bird, you can plan accordingly.

Generally speaking, ½ cup is considered a proper serving of vegetables and side dishes, and such desserts as puddings and ice creams. (If I offered my grandchildren ½ cup of spaghetti topped with a tablespoon of sauce, they'd drum me out of the regiment. But never mind—½ cup is the convention, and ½ cup it stands.) Again, ½ cup is considered a proper serving of a soup such as consommé that begins the meal; however, if the soup is essentially the main dish, such as a chowder served at supper with only a bread and a salad to accompany it, 1 cup or 1¼ cups is considered a serving. When it comes to meat, count on four servings to the pound of boneless meat, two to three of meat with some bone, and only one serving per pound of heavily boned meat, such as short ribs. Some foods, such as eggs, can mercifully be counted by the piece. With some, you must take into consideration the surroundings: Is the food served with a sauce on toast or in a patty case, for example?

There is a rule—which, like most rules, doesn't work out more than half the time—for determining the number of servings in a given dish: Total the ingredients in cupfuls, multiply by 2, and the answer is the number of servings. Thus, a casserole dish calling for 2 cups chopped chicken, 2 cups leftover stuffing, 1 cup chicken gravy, 1 cup green beans, and ½ cup slivered almonds totals 6½ cups. That makes 13 servings—right? Wrong. The almonds are garnish, and don't count. The gravy will combine, in cooking, with the chicken and stuffing and swell their total by only a small amount. Very well, 5 cups, then, or 10 servings? Technically, yes; practically, no. Consider the dish in your mind's eye and you'll arrive at 6 generous, but not overgenerous, servings. This is the main dish of a meal, remember.

Indeed, your mind's eye and your common sense are your best tools in determining yield. An angel food cake cuts into 16 miserly servings, or 14 more generous ones, or 12 whoppers. If dessert is going to be angel food cake with ice cream, 16 is ample; for angel food cake alone, 14 is fine, particularly if the cake is glazed or to be served with a sauce; if totally unadorned, better make it 12.

COMPONENTS OF A WELL-WRITTEN RECIPE

A *PORT AND WALNUT RABBIT*

B *Makes 4 servings*

C Wensleydale is a pale, flaky British cheese with a pungent flavor and an assertive odor.

D Walnut Toast (see below)
E 4 cups (about 1 pound) shredded wensleydale cheese F
2 tablespoons all-purpose flour
⅔ cup port wine
½ cup heavy or whipping cream
2 tablespoons butter or margarine
2 teaspoons worcestershire sauce
1 teaspoon dry mustard
⅛ teaspoon red (cayenne) pepper
2 egg yolks
2 firm-ripe tomatoes, each cut in 4 wedges G

H
Set out 4 ungreased 10-ounce ramekins or other small dishes. Prepare Walnut Toast; set aside. Into bottom of double boiler, pour water 2 inches deep; bring to a simmer over medium heat. In top of double boiler, toss cheese and flour together until cheese is coated. Add wine, cream, butter, worcestershire, mustard, and pepper. Set over simmering water; stir until thickened. Remove from heat. Stir in egg yolks until well blended. Divide mixture evenly among the 4 ramekins. Place 2 tomato wedges opposite each other on each

serving; stand 2 toast triangles between tomatoes. Serve at once. Pass remaining toast. Refrigerate leftovers, covered. J

I *Variations:* Substitute cheddar cheese, sharp or mellow, for the wensleydale. Substitute Madeira or sherry for the port; if a nonalcoholic version is desired, substitute unsweetened apple juice for the wine.

K

Walnut Toast

8 slices thin white bread, crusts removed

10 tablespoons butter OR margarine, at room temperature, divided

½ cup ground black OR english walnuts

L

Place bread on wax paper. Using 8 tablespoons of the butter, spread both sides of each bread slice. Divide nuts over one side of each slice, pressing nuts gently into bread. Place 2 slices of bread together, walnuts between, to make 4 sandwiches; cut diagonally. In small skillet, melt remaining 2 tablespoons butter. Sauté sandwiches until golden. Cut diagonally once more.

LEGEND, COMPONENTS OF A WELL-WRITTEN RECIPE

A Recipe title

B Yield

C	Comment
D	Reference to subsidiary recipe
E	Ingredients
F	Turnover line
G	Preparation included in list of ingredients
H	Method
I	Variations
J	Storage information
K	Subsidiary recipe: title, ingredients, method
L	Note that when a choice of ingredients is given, the word *or* which separates them is lower case if the choice will not affect the flavor or texture of the dish, but is carried in upper case (OR) when the flavor or texture will be affected by the choice.

Ingredients

These should be listed strictly in order of use. If, for example, there are onions to be sautéed in butter, list the butter and then the onions, because the butter must first be placed in the pan and melted before the onions can be added to it. The only allowable departure from this rule is when a commercial cookbook sponsor insists that his product be listed first, even if it is the last item into the pot.

Method

This, the manner in which the dish should be assembled, should follow the list of ingredients exactly, and should be written in simple, clear terms.

Necessary Information

Under this heading fall the useful bits and pieces that can make or break a recipe. They include cooking time(s) and temperature(s), both oven and stovetop, as well as setting if the dish is to be—or can be—cooked by microwave; nature and size of utensil(s) and equipment used in preparation and in cooking; preparation of cooking pan(s); preheating of oven to proper temperature. All of these elements should be specified. If the finished dish is to be cooked in the oven, specify preheating temperature and size and preparation of baking pan (greasing or not, flouring or not) at the beginning of the recipe, sizes of other equipment as you come to each. The exception is preheating for a dish that takes longer than fifteen minutes to prepare, such as various breads and rolls; in these cases, specify preheating at a point about fifteen minutes ahead of the time the food will be ready to put into the oven.

Other Elements

As well as the preceding essentials, recipes may—at the author's option, or the editor's, or the book designer's—carry one or several of the following useful extra elements.

COMMENT. A line or two of added information, positioned either above or more commonly below the recipe title. A comment might tell the cook that the recipe is quick and easy, that it is a make-ahead, that it is not recommended for preparation on a hot and/or humid day, or it might offer the country of origin of the dish from which this one is adapted—

anything that will add to the knowledge and pleasure of the cook.

GARNISHES. These are almost always optional. They should appear at the end of the ingredients list as "parsley sprigs, if desired" or "parsley sprigs (optional)" and reappear at the appropriate place in the method as "Garnish with parsley sprigs, if desired."

STORAGE. State whether the food should be stored at room temperature or refrigerated, loosely or tightly covered, and in what sort of container. If it may be frozen, say so. If it must be refrigerated until serving time, say so. If it should be stored in glass or pottery, because of high acidity, tell the reader. For room-temperature or refrigerator storage, state approximate length of time. Any or all of this information should be positioned at the end of the recipe.

VARIATION. This, or more than one of these, rings changes on the basic recipe, as "One jar of baby-food puréed prunes may be substituted for the chopped cooked prunes in this recipe," or "If hickory nuts are not available, substitute walnuts." Or you may suggest something that will change the flavor and/or texture considerably, as "Another time, try this with banana. Omit chopped cranberries. Stir 1 cup well-mashed banana and, if desired, ½ cup chopped pecans, into the batter just before placing in the pan." Variations should be so labeled, and appear separately, just following the recipe to which they apply.

SERVING SUGGESTIONS. These offer embellishments to "dress up" the recipe, as "For a more elaborate dessert, top each slice of cake with about 2 tablespoons sliced, sweetened strawberries, and spoon English Custard (page 124) over all," or "For a heartier dish, sprinkle each serving with croutons, then with shredded sharp cheddar cheese." This kind of information should be positioned separate from, but immediately following, the recipe to which it applies.

MENU SUGGESTIONS. Tell the reader about something, or several somethings, that goes particularly well with the dish, as "Serve with baked sweet potatoes, Spicy Apple Rings (page 38), and buttered green beans." Again, this information should be positioned separate from, but immediately following, the recipe. Alternatively, if the cookbook is so designed, complete menus incorporating at least some of the foods in the book can appear as a separate item (with page references), just preceding each recipe—you'll find that this approach can become pretty awkward—or as a part of the introduction to each section of the book, incorporating recipes in the forthcoming section. Or menus may be offered as an entirely separate section.

TIPS. These are bits of information that apply not only to the recipe(s) near which they are positioned, but also to cooking in general. For example, "If possible, prepare breaded foods at least two hours in advance of cooking. Store uncovered, in a single layer, in the refrigerator. You will find that the breading will adhere much better than if the food is cooked immediately after preparation." Tips should be positioned, preferably boxed or otherwise set off, on the same page as or the page facing a recipe to which the information applies.

NUTRITIONAL INFORMATION. Total calorie counts and/or separate-item nutritional values (general, or in reference to RDA) are useful additional information to supply the reader, particularly in cookbooks that make some claim to assisting the cook in preparing well-balanced family meals. Position immediately following each recipe, preferably set in italics or boldface or otherwise distinguished from the recipe itself.

SUBSIDIARY RECIPE. If one or more is to be used, refer to it at the proper point in the list of ingredients, as "Fudge Frosting (below)," and "Frost with Fudge Frosting between the layers and on top and sides of cake," in the method. The subsidiary recipe should then be positioned immediately following the main one. Alternatively, particularly if the subsidiary recipe is for a food that can be used with other recipes as well, it may be grouped with other, similar recipes in a separate section, such as a group of frostings following a group of cakes, or a group of sauces following a group of main or side dishes. If subsidiary recipes are grouped, the appropriate page number should accompany the reference in the main recipe.

The watchword for all these optional additions to recipes is consistency. That doesn't mean that if you offer a variation or whatever with one recipe you must offer one with all the rest, but neither should you give only one or two variations throughout the entire book. If you give menus in one place, they should appear elsewhere, too.

Sometimes writers invent a whole new nomenclature for these optionals—variations become "Another way," menu suggestions are "Goes well with," tips are "Good to know," and so on. Provided the phrases are not too cute, and provided they fit well with the tone of the book, there's nothing wrong with this practice. But again, you must be consistent. If you make "To gild the lily" your synonym for serving suggestions (and I sincerely hope that you won't), all serving suggestions throughout the book must be tagged in the same way so the reader can locate them readily and know at once, each time he or she sees the phrase, what type of help is being offered.

Terms and Turns of Phrase

Unless you are doing a commercial cookbook, you will want to call most ingredients by their common names. However, a very special ingredient, the exact duplication of which is critical to the recipe, may require clues to guide the reader, or even an exact identification.

In most cases, a general wording using a common name serves the purpose:

2 (9-ounce) packages frozen peas

If you wish the small frozen peas to be used, say:

2 (9-ounce) packages tiny frozen peas

If you feel that only a certain brand—C&R, for example—will do, call for:

2 (9-ounce) packages frozen petite peas

Here you are using a generic term (in the cookbook sense, not by dictionary definition), which is supposed to indicate to the reader exactly which product is to be used without calling it by brand name. The drawback is that at least half your readers won't have the foggiest notion of what you're getting at.

Worse, C&R peas may not be distributed throughout the country but, hopefully, your book will be.

In the case of small frozen peas, it's not going to matter overmuch which brand the reader chooses to use. But in cases where the exact ingredient is critical, use the commercial name so that no one can accuse you of being obscure.

Generic names are chosen by manufacturers for their products. For example:

Post Grape-Nuts	=	malted cereal granules
Instant Yuban Coffee	=	instant premium blended coffee
S.O.S. Soap Pads	=	oval blue soap pads
Kraft Natural Caraway Cheese	=	natural caraway spiced cheese

As you can see, these aren't very revealing. However, most companies have available lists of the generics approved for their products. If you want such a list, write to the publicity or consumer relations department of a company and ask for their approved generic terms; they'll be happy to fill your request.

From time to time, commercial names of food products will undergo a change. For example, for many years Worcestershire Sauce was a trade name, owned by Lea & Perrins. If you wished to use the sauce as a recipe ingredient, you were supposed to capitalize it:

1 tablespoon Worcestershire Sauce

Several years ago, Lea & Perrins' rights to exclusive use of the name ran out. Now French's, Crosse & Blackwell and several other companies make the sauce (each according to its own recipe), and the ingredients listing can now look like this:

1 tablespoon worcestershire sauce

But wait a minute—Worcestershire is the name of a shire (county) in England. Doesn't it then require a capital letter as a geographical place name even though no longer as a trade name? Not according to the rules followed by some good cookbook writers and editors and their publishing houses. They—and I am unalterably one of them—prefer to lowercase in cookbook usage terms that require a capital when they refer to geographical areas. This cookbook styling says that cooking terms, such as "french fried," and utensil names, such as "dutch oven," shall not be capitalized. When you write your cookbook, the choice is yours; when it is sold, the choice will be up to the publishing house copy editor, who follows the house style sheet.

The matter of when, and when not, to capitalize can become very sticky. Cheese names are a case in point. More often than not, Parmesan carries a capital letter because the writer or the copy editor believes it to be a geographical place name. Not true. The place is Parma, the cheese is parmesan. Likewise, the place is Rome (or Roma, if you happen to be there), the cheese is romano. Cheddar is a place name, but there are other terms connected with the cheese that derive from the name—"the cheddaring process" and "a cheese that is cheddared." If you use "Cheddaring" and "Cheddared" and other such terms in a like manner, your book's pages are going to be as spotted with capital letters as a child with chicken pox, an undesirable look. But if you use upper-case Cheddar and lower-case cheddaring, you are constructing a trap into which, on some other occasion, you may fall with a thud—and, worse, have to go back through the entire manuscript, upper-casing or lower-casing dozens of words. And so, although I have never agreed with him in general, I say, along with Karl Marx, down with capitalism!

There are certain turns of phrase that cookbook writers like to use and that cookbook readers like to find, because they are familiar and familiarity breeds content. Home cooks, especially those without full-fledged confidence in their culinary skills, feel reassured and comfortable with phrasing they are used to, ways of saying things that have worked well in the past.

Whatever familiar usages you prefer, as a cookbook writer you are obligated to phrase any instruction exactly the same way each time you use it within the confines of a single book. For example, in a bread recipe, you may tell the cook to:

> Place dough in a buttered bowl; turn to butter on all sides. Cover lightly with a clean, dry towel. Let rise in a warm place, free from drafts, until doubled in bulk, about 1 hour.

In each other bread recipe in the book, that set of instructions should be worded in the same way, with variations only in whether or not the dough should be covered and in the time that the rising will take. The same is true of all instructions, from simple to complicated. A recipe is the wrong place to think up fresh, new ways in which to couch tired old terms.

While we're on the subject of bread recipes, unless your cookbook is for an audience of old-hand bread bakers, you'll be well advised to define some of the terms used in this class of recipe. Clump such definitions in one place—in the introduction, perhaps, or in a boxed or otherwise set-off list near the front of the book. Otherwise, you're going to have to do a lot of defining in each recipe—and bread recipes are long enough without this—or leave the cook to fight his or her way through alone. Among the terms that need defining for amateur bakers are *proof, knead, punch down, rest, rise, double in bulk, shape into loaves.* Likewise, you'll do well to explain other facets of bread-making that may be unfamiliar: the nature of yeast (that it is alive, that it is easily killed), differences between yeast breads and quick breads, between kneaded and batter breads, how refrigerator-raise methods work, how to obtain the kind of crust desired (buttering, brushing with water, brushing with egg wash, etc.), how to tell when the bread is done.

In the same way, overall explanations of terms used in any group of recipes in which the home cook may be unfamiliar with ingredients and/or methods is a wise move. Repeated explanations are tedious for both writer and reader and result in recipes of unwieldy length. But even repeated explanations are better than none at all, for that way lies frustration for the cook—and for you indignant letters complaining, "I tried your rotten Butterscotch Angelfood and it fell flat on its face!"

Another area that requires attention is the answer to the question that inexperienced cooks ask most often: "How do I know when it's done?" Because of the wide range of when-it's-done signs, that one needs to be dealt with recipe by recipe.

You will, of course, give an exact oven temperature and a reasonably exact stovetop temperature, such as "Cook over low heat" or "Sauté over medium heat," and so on. If you also give a clue to the appearance of the food when it is properly cooked, plus an approximate time (it's dangerous, considering the variation among stoves, to give an arbitrary, exact time), you will have solved the cook's problems.

"Bake until golden brown and the cake shrinks from the edge of the pan, about 30 minutes" will give the cook enough clues upon which to base his or her judgment. So will ". . . until evenly browned and a wooden pick inserted in the center comes out clean, about 45 minutes," or ". . . until onions are transparent but not browned, 6 to 8 minutes," or any other phrases that offer both the appearance of the food in question and a range of time that the cooking process should take.

There are many other set phrases commonly used to clue the home cook, such as "Chill until the mixture reaches the consistency of unbeaten egg white, 30 to 45 minutes," or "brown sugar, firmly packed," or "Cook, stirring constantly, over hot, not boiling water," or "Beat until stiff but not dry," or "Beat until thick and pale, at least 5 minutes with an electric mixer or 15 minutes or more by hand." These are only a few of the dozens of such phrases. If you are a good cook, such phrases are familiar to you. (If they aren't, why are you reading this book?)

Our old friend convention believes that home cooks have very delicate sensibilities. They are thought to be revolted by unpleasant concepts, by terms that bring ugly pictures to mind. Thus, in cookbooks you skim the foam, or sometimes the froth, but never the scum, from a cooking soup or stew; you place a dollop, not a blob, of whipped cream atop a serving of dessert; you remove, not dig out, the seeds of a tomato or a citrus fruit. There are many of these, but they are not hard to cope with. Just be refined, be constantly a lady or gentleman, and you'll be safe.

Shortcuts That Work, Shortcuts That Don't

Whether or not to abbreviate terms in a recipe has been the subject of numerous long-winded debates for years. If you are putting together a very short, very space-saving collection of recipes, such as for a pamphlet to accompany a food product, there is no room for argument—you must abbreviate, and it's up to the reader to make sense of the information given. But when you deal with the normal, average cookbook, you can abbreviate or not as you choose. There are no hard-and-fast rules. Some writers abbreviate everything, some nothing. Some would prefer not to abbreviate, but find that the style guidelines of the publishing house to which they've sold a book require a certain amount of abbreviation. A piece of heartfelt advice: If there is a choice, opt for very few abbreviations or none at all. That way the printed page looks better (less spotty and choppy) and there is no way that the reader can misread or misinterpret you.

Common sense militates against abbreviating two terms that can easily be, in their abbreviated condition, mistaken for one another or misread in the once-over-lightly of a cook who is pressed for time. Such a pair are "teaspoon" and "tablespoon": *tsp.* and *tbsp.* are too much alike; *t.* and *T.* can also be confused. Although *c.* is sometimes used, "cup" is so short a word it seems ridiculous to abbreviate it. On the other hand, *oz.* for "ounce," *pkg.* for "package," *env.* for "envelope," *lb.* for "pound"—and there are others—work well enough, if abbreviate you must.

One abbreviation is constantly used in all kinds of cookbooks, and has been for many years: F for "Fahrenheit." Indeed, some cookbooks omit the F entirely, simply stating "Preheat oven to 350°" or even "Preheat to 350." On the opposite side from omitting it entirely, the small superior °

that stands for "degrees" is sometimes spelled out, as in "Preheat oven to 350 degrees" or "to 350 degrees F." The cookbook sorority used to argue, quite reasonably, that because oven temperature couldn't be confused with anything else, it was therefore okay to express it any way you wanted to. But that was before metric raised its head and we were faced with C as in Celsius, as well as F as in Fahrenheit. When (if) kitchen measurements come to metric (which is tantamount, among cookbook writers, to the inflammatory phrase "When push comes to shove"), we'll have a whole new area of traps into which the unwary can fall. If a cooking temperature is expressed in C when it should have been F, or the other way around, the cook is truly in the soup, for these numbers on the thermometer are far apart.

In the middle of the last decade, when we felt the hot breath of metric on our necks, some of us took to offering both cooking temperatures, on the principle of better safe than sorry. To further complicate matters, because an even F temperature seldom has an even C equivalent, we rounded off the expression of C to the nearest number ending in zero or five. Thus, for a while a great many cookbooks expressed oven temperature as:

> Preheat oven to 350° F (175° C).

If that makes you uneasy, pity the poor British cookbook writers, also in the throes of metrification, who had to say:

> Preheat oven to 350° F (175° C, gas mark 5).

However, when the hoo-hah over metric died down somewhat (among their many other divergent and often obscure opinions, Democrats are metric boosters, Republicans are not), most cookbook writers dropped the practice of expressing C temperatures.

Of course, oven temperatures expressed in Celsius were not the only problems that rode in on metric's coattails; there were new measurements of a number of kinds, each with its own abbreviation. Cooks and cookbook writers who had attended European cooking schools (but not British ones—they constitute a whole other ballgame) already knew metric measurements and were familiar with their usage, but all the rest were left with their mouths hanging open and a sudden urge to look for an alternative way to earn a living. A raft of books and pamphlets appeared on the market, making clear (but not very) all this new information. Kids learned metric—easily, as kids do—in school, and turned the tables by rushing home to help with their mothers' homework. Manufacturers buried cookbookers under a snowstorm of conversion tables and metric-calibrated measuring cups and spoons, thermometers, rulers, and tape measures. Many cookbook publishers decided to come down on the side of too much information rather than not enough and crammed all the measurements of both kinds into each recipe, to the point where it became difficult to tell the players even with a program. To give you an idea, here are a few of the ingredients and a couple of lines from the method of a cookbook I wrote during the Great Metric Scare:

1 can (8 oz./226 g) tomato sauce
500 ml (2 cups) chopped cooked chicken
.5 ml (⅛ teaspoon) crushed red pepper flakes
375 ml (1½ cups) shredded mild cheddar cheese

Butter an 8- or 9-inch (20–23 cm) baking pan and a 1½ quart (1.5 liter) casserole. . . . Reserve ½ cup (125 ml) cheese for top layer. Bake at 375° F (190° C) 30 to 35 minutes.

Note that *oz.*, the abbreviation for "ounces," carries a period, but *g* for "grams" and *ml* for "milliliter" do not. This is because convention says that the metric abbreviations do not carry periods, and the copy editor at the publishing house that put out the book was not about to fly in the face of convention; however, the style sheet of the publishing house called for periods after *lb.*, *oz.*, and other such abbreviations in food-related text, and she wasn't about to fly in the face of that rule, either. So what we ended up with was a mishmash calculated to scare any cook right out of the kitchen and any cookbooker right out of the profession. (Indeed, I was so shaken by the experience that I hastily got myself a job as a fiction editor and didn't write a word for over a year.)

It finally dawned on the cookbook trade, however, that inasmuch as in recipes we had been measuring by the piece (2 eggs, 1 clove garlic) or by the cupful or multiples or fractions thereof, or by the tablespoon or multiples or fractions thereof, all of which had no conceptual relationship to metric, there was no reason that we couldn't go right on doing so, thereby saving ourselves and the American cook from the funny farm.

Gradually, metric fell away. It came to the happy point at which an editor called me one day to ask if I could put together a breakfast and brunch cookbook.

"Sure," I told him, then added timidly, "metric?"

"Metric? No. Forget metric."

I did so gladly. For the time being, that is. Metric will return (probably the next time the Democrats come up to bat) and will have to be dealt with. Cans and packages still express their contents in metric as well as in the more familiar pounds and ounces. Liquor is sold nowadays in bottles containing a liter, or increments or fractions thereof, rather than by the gallon or quart or pint or that no-man's-land measurement, the fifth. That's because the liquor business rushed to comply with the new directives and then, when the metric rug was pulled out from under them, found it "economically unfeasible" to retool and start over a second time.

Measurements and Modifications

As well as carefully stating amounts of ingredients in a recipe that you are writing, the manner in which you state those amounts can be very important—can, indeed, make all the difference between an easy-to-use cookbook and one that is so difficult to understand that the home cook's desire is to set fire to it.

Here are three simple ways to state the same ingredient:

1 (6-ounce) can tomato paste
1 can (6 ounces) tomato paste
1 can tomato paste, 6 ounces

All three are acceptable, depending upon what editor you are dealing with. Indeed, there is a fourth way that many editors use, but with which I disagree:

1 6-ounce can tomato paste

It is altogether too easy to read that as "16-ounce can"; in fact, sometimes the typesetter sends it back reading that way. The proofreader, whose hobby is macramé, not cooking, accepts it. The author, checking proofs, lets it slip by. Thus an error is perpetuated, and no amount of breast-beating and cries of *mea culpa* can snatch it back once it's printed. Of the other three ways to list ingredients that call for a can or package size, I much prefer the first. It states the elements in logical order, and the parentheses keep the statement clear. The second serves reasonably well when you are dealing with only one; with two or more you're in trouble, as:

2 cans (6 ounces each) tomato paste

This makes a longer line, although what is meant is perfectly clear. However, the other alternative—doubling the number of ounces, so that you offer the sum of two cans (12 ounces)—is not acceptable. It's too confusing, and could be interpreted as calling for two 12-ounce cans; if tomato paste were not available in 12-ounce cans, this manner of statement might be marginally acceptable, but 12-ounce cans are available—and if the cook uses two of them, he or she is going to have a failed recipe and a fit of temper.

Picky? You bet! On a firm foundation of picky are good cookbooks built.

There is a way of stating virtually every ingredient used in cooking that is not so much a matter of right vs. wrong as of good vs. bad or, at the least, best vs. not-so-dandy.

If an ingredient is to be modified in any way (thawed, melted, scalded, beaten, etc.) or if it requires special preparation (peeled, diced, grated, chopped, etc.), that information should be included in the list of ingredients rather than in the method. Not only does this save space and excessive verbiage in the method, but it can also avoid some of the problems cookbooks are heir to. Home cooks are inclined to read over the list of ingredients before starting to prepare a recipe, to make certain they have everything necessary on hand. But few read the method, except for true kitchen novices who are afraid to stop and mop their brows unless the cookbook says it's okay. Thus the ingredient

1 (9-ounce) package frozen chopped spinach, thawed

will save the cook, who has the oven preheating, the pan greased, and the roulade partially mixed, from discovering at that late point that the brick-hard package of spinach must relax before it can be used. For the same reasons, because an efficient, methodical cook assembles all the ingredients before actual preparation of the dish begins, those ingredients should be peeled, chopped, mashed, sifted, diced, dissolved, shredded, or whatever else needs to be done to them during the preliminary assembly period, not one at a time throughout the preparation.

Another cogent reason for giving the modifications that must be made in the list of ingredients is that it results in accurate measurements. Consider these two ingredient specifications:

1 cup blanched almonds, ground
1 cup ground blanched almonds

The same? Not at all. A moment's thought will lead you to realize that there is a considerable—and probably critical—difference between almonds measured before and after grinding. About ¼ to ⅓ cup, as a matter of fact, sufficient to make or break a dish. As a writer of recipes, it's up to you to be aware of such differences and to make certain that you call for exactly what you mean.

There are many related measurements and modifications that are merely silly, as:

½ cup green pepper, chopped

How do you measure ½ cup green pepper before you chop —or mince or dice—it, or in some other manner render it measurable? The same is true of all other bulky ingredients; they must be modified before they can be measured.

For reasons of saving time, modifications of other kinds should also appear in the ingredients list. Milk to be scalded can be put on the stove while the cook assembles the other ingredients. Butter can be melted. Vegetables can be peeled and cut up, as necessary. Garlic can be peeled and minced or slivered or pressed. Eggs can be separated; whole eggs or egg yolks can be beaten. And there are dozens more such preparations that are better made before the actual assembling of the dish begins.

Measurements should be stated in common, basic terms that the home cook can readily understand and for which the average home kitchen supplies measuring tools. No pinches, please—a pinch may indeed be "the amount of a substance that can be picked up between the ends of the thumb and forefinger," but suppose my thumb and forefinger are much larger than yours? No dashes, no little bits, no butter the size of a walnut, no handfuls of flour, no teacups, no soup spoons—nothing that is not an expression of an amount that can be measured with a standard kitchen measuring tool. No cubes or sticks of butter either, please, unless at the same time stated in some other terms as well, as:

1 stick (½ cup) butter

It may come as a blow to some people's feelings of regional chauvinism, but butter is not uniformly packed in sticks and/or cubes. Sticks are more common in the East, cubes in the West—and goodness knows what's gone on in the middle of the country since I shook its dust off my shoes. You may feel that any fool should know that the quarter-pound of butter neatly wrapped to separate it from its neighbors is either a stick or a cube (which isn't really a cube, but a shorter, fatter stick). Not true. I have been asked many times, "How do I measure a cube of butter? Is it about a third of a stick?" So don't say I didn't warn you.

Likewise, don't call for hard-to-arrive-at measurements. You may know that ⅙ cup is half of ⅓ cup, but your reader may have been home with the measles when they discussed division of fractions in school. You may know that there are 4 tablespoons to ¼ cup and that, therefore, if you measure a full cup of flour and then remove 2 tablespoons you'll arrive at the called-for ⅞ cup, but don't count on the reader having the same knowledge; if you must use ⅞ cup, call for "1 cup less 2 tablespoons."

Some ingredients are always, by convention, called for or modified or both by the use of a convenient phrase that everyone understands, or at least is supposed to. When you call for sugar, you are assumed to mean granulated sugar; all others —light brown, dark brown, granulated brown, liquid brown, powdered (or confectioners)—must be called for by their full names. Brown sugar is always packed, for the logical reason that, loosely spooned into a cup, it does not provide the quantity the recipe requires. Hard cheese—parmesan, sap sago, romano, and the like—is properly called for as grated; softer cheeses—cheddar, jack, swiss—are called for as shredded (if you've ever tried to grate cheddar, you know why); crumbly cheeses, such as bleu, are called for as crumbled, simply because it is impossible either to grate or shred them.

When you call for ingredients difficult to work with when they are fresh from the refrigerator, such as butter or cream cheese, list:

1 (8-ounce) package cream cheese, at room temperature

Room temperature serves nicely—unless you are dealing with an eccentric cook who keeps the kitchen at fifty degrees—but no one can be expected to cover *all* the bases. Why not call for softened butter or cheese? Because cooks have been known to melt it, pound it, cut it into tiny pieces and otherwise commit mayhem in order to soften it, which makes a lot of extra work and in some cases affects the outcome of the recipe.

Eggs are one of those blessed ingredients that can be called for by the piece and consequently should not be liable to misinterpretation. The convention of

2 eggs, separated

should cause no trouble—break the eggs, put the whites in one container, the yolks in a second, and there you are. On the other hand:

2 eggs, divided

is something else again. That term, often used in cookbooks, means that one portion of that ingredient is used at one place in the recipe, the other portion(s) in another place or other places. Here, in the case of eggs, one egg might be used in the dough of a bread, the second to make egg wash with which to brush the top of the bread to produce a handsome, glossy finish. Many ingredients—flour, sugar, butter, and others—may be labeled "divided" in a list of ingredients; the method, then, should make the uses of the divided ingredient clear. Suppose the divided ingredient is 1 cup of flour; the method should direct: "Combine sugar and ½ cup of the flour"; and later, "Fold in remaining ½ cup of flour." The alternative to this method is to specify the exact amount of flour, or whatever, in its proper (order of use) place in the ingredients list, even though this may require specifying flour at two, or even three or four, places in the list. Either method offers possibilities for confusion, but the second invites far more errors than the first.

Back to eggs for a moment. Separated yolks and whites, particularly whites, beat up to optimum volume when they are at room temperature. (However, they separate more readily when they are straight from the refrigerator.) Optimum volume is almost always a virtue in any recipe, but in some—angel food, for instance—it is an absolute necessity. In such cases, specify room temperature when you list the eggs as an ingredient. Another eggs convention is size. Recipes are developed—or are supposed to be—using large eggs. When you specify eggs in your ingredients list, you are understood to be calling for large eggs; if you want small, or extra-large, or jumbo, you'll have to say so.

One last word on eggs. You are often directed in a recipe to beat egg yolks until they are "thick and lemon colored."

Thick, yes; lemon colored, no. Look at those thick yolks. They are a light yellow-orange, how light depending on the deepness of color of the yolks before beating. That is not the color of a lemon. A lot of novice cooks have gone on beating egg yolks long past the point of no return, waiting for them to magically turn the color of a lemon. They never did, of course, and these novices are now the most enthusiastic patrons of take-out food emporiums. When beaten yolks are properly *thick*, they are also properly *pale.* The direction "Beat until thick and pale" covers the situation exactly. Forget the lemons.

This seems like a good place to point out that if you require several modifications for one ingredient, you'll be best served by holding back one or more for the method. An ingredient list that calls for

> *3 eggs, at room temperature, divided, separated*

is enough to drive the most sober-minded soul to the cooking sherry.

Which brings us neatly to beer, wine, liquor, and liqueurs: to use or not to use? If you are doing a "gourmet" cookbook, there is no problem; you can add spirits wherever required without hesitation. At other levels, however, things can get a bit sticky. If you are preparing a cookbook for old-line Methodists, you would be wise to ignore the fact that spirits exist. If you suspect that there are those in your audience who frown on the use of intoxicating beverages, offer a substitute: Fruit juices, particularly apple juice, work well in some recipes, stock or broth in others. But unless you are doing a cookbook totally concerned with the use of spirits in cooking, don't have recourse to the bottle in every recipe; oddly enough, there are a lot of people who have no objection to liquor as a libation but dislike the flavor in food. Common sense, as in everything else, should be your guide here.

At first blush, it's difficult to see how so simple and ordinary an ingredient as water could cause controversy, but in truth it has been the subject of assorted arguments among cookbookers for years. (If you are beginning to think that cookbook writers spend more time arguing than writing, you could be right. We're a contentious bunch.) There is a school of thought that says that water, because it can be assumed to be available in every home kitchen, should *never* be listed as an ingredient. An opposed school holds that water, like any other ingredient, should *always* be listed. And there is the middle-of-the-road group that contends that plain old out-of-the-tap water should not be listed, but modified water (boiling, ice water, at a particular temperature as for proofing yeast or softening gelatin) must appear as an ingredient. Choose any one of these three positions. But once you've chosen, stick to it. Calling for water in some cases and not in others within the same book will confuse everyone, including you.

Another area where modification is usually required is herbs/spices/seasonings/flavorings. Herbs are available dried or fresh; it is necessary to specify which, because the two are interchangeable in flavor but not in amount—about three times as much of the prepared (minced, snipped, shredded) fresh herb is required to give the same flavor intensity as the dried. Spices are usually available in more than one form: cinnamon as both ground and sticks (rolls of bark), cardamom as ground and pods, mace as ground and blade, nutmeg and allspice as ground and whole, and so on. Cookbook convention says that if you call for a spice in teaspoon fractions or increments, you mean the ground spice; if you wish the other form, it is necessary to say so, as:

1 (3-inch) stick cinnamon, broken in 3 pieces

Pepper is available in many forms: ground white, red, and black (black is further subdivided into fine, medium, and coarse grinds); whole dried peppercorns, both white and black; dried red pepper flakes (often with some of the small, yellow seeds); whole green peppercorns or whole or sliced hot peppers bottled in vinegar or oil; and, of course, fresh peppers of several kinds are available in produce sections. Convention says that if a recipe calls merely for pepper, ground black pepper is meant; all other kinds must be specified. Convention once said that if you wished ground red pepper, you specified cayenne in the list of ingredients. That is in the process of change; now we specify:

⅛ teaspoon ground red (cayenne) pepper

and shortly we will drop the explanatory "cayenne" and simply call for ground red pepper. Finally, there are several kinds of blow-your-head-off hot pepper sauces, the most familiar—and most widely available—of which is Tabasco, a trade name. These should be called for by the drop in recipes, which goes against the rule that states that ingredients be measured only by standard kitchen measuring instruments; in this case, 1/16 teaspoon, the smallest of those measurements, may be too much, so we resort to drops.

Such seasonings as lemon juice, A-1 Sauce, soy sauce, and others of that ilk are generally called for by the teaspoon or tablespoon. Be certain that your readers will know what it is you are specifying. If you call for hoisin sauce, for example, in a non-Chinese, nongourmet cookbook, you will need to explain (in a note) what it is and that it may be purchased in Oriental markets.

Flavoring extracts offer few problems. If you call for

1 teaspoon vanilla extract

in the list of ingredients, simply say "Add vanilla" in the method and you're home free. Be aware, though, that there are a number of spice-flavored extracts and a few exotic ones. The spice-flavored extracts are for use in delicate dishes where the ground spice might show up as a collection of off-putting specks or blobs, and they serve that purpose very well. The exotics—banana, pistachio, coconut, and a number of others—are meant to take the place of a large quantity of the item whose flavor they reproduce in dishes where such a quantity is not desirable; also, they are much more intense in flavor than the nut or berry or fruit or whatever itself. Rum and brandy extracts are also available, to be used where a large quantity of the liquor might liquify the food too much, or in foods for teetotalers who nevertheless enjoy the flavor. In a cookbook for skilled, experienced cooks, you are justified in calling for anything the recipe requires, including any off-beat flavoring extract. But in a cookbook for the novice, or in a budget book, you're better off avoiding these: They are both expensive and often hard to come by.

The kind of flour to be used in a recipe is another area where specification is required. Once recipes simply called for "flour" and let it go at that, but no more. Various flours are widely available, and can be called for in recipes without causing the home cook undue hardship. If you mean plain white wheat flour, call for all-purpose flour. Or specify self-rising, pastry, bread, cake, granular, or unbleached flour if you wish to. Whole-wheat and rye flours are easily come by, too; while these were once confined to cookbooks on baking, any general cookbook can now specify them. Even rice, tritacale, potato, and corn flours are available in some supermarkets and in most health food stores.

Dealing With the Method

Once the ingredients list is on paper in its proper order, the method follows as the night the day. Clarity and simplicity are the watchwords, but don't come down so hard on the side of simplicity that the home cook must have a sideline of mind reading to follow you. You'll certainly specify the items discussed earlier in this section, such as cooking times and temperatures, but also don't forget sizes of bowls and pans, kinds of utensils. Such phrases as "small bowl of electric mixer," "a medium bowl," "large saucepan," "small, heavy saucepan," "wooden spoon," "slotted spoon," and so on are conventional ones and explain themselves.

There is a fine line between saying too much and saying too little; with practice you will learn to walk it gracefully.

In setting up recipes and typing them, use the simplest possible style: title, followed by ingredients typed as a double-spaced, single-column list, followed in turn by the method. The clearest way of presenting the method is in numbered steps, as:

1. Preheat oven to 350° F. Grease and flour a 10-inch tube pan; set aside.

2. In large bowl of electric mixer, cream together butter and sugar at low speed until mixture is light and fluffy.
3. Add eggs one at a time, beating well after each addition. Beat in vanilla.

Unfortunately, few cookbooks other than those that are quite lavishly produced can afford the space that the numbered-steps method occupies. There is nothing, however, to prevent you from using this easy-read form when you put together a first cookbook, as yet unsold. Once you have sold the book, the editor will tell you in what manner he or she wants the recipes presented.

The alternative to the step-by-step presentation is to type the method in double-spaced paragraphs; a single paragraph will do if the method is brief, but if it's quite long, break into two or three or even more paragraphs. At the least, open with a brief paragraph that encompasses preparation: preheating oven if required, preparing pan, offering any instructions for preparation of ingredients that were too long or complicated to include in the ingredients list. Follow with one or two or more paragraphs dealing with the method of putting the dish together. Conclude with a sum-up paragraph telling the home cook how long to bake or cook, by what signs he or she will be able to tell when the dish is done, how to cool, how to store, and the yield.

Be prepared, incidentally, for possible flak on the subject of preheating ovens. When we first became aware of the energy crunch, a number of people—particularly those who didn't understand the chemistry of cooking—pointed out that preheating an oven was a waste of energy: ten to fifteen minutes of turned-on heat with nothing in the big, empty oven to make use of it! After a number of baking failures, such as pale and soggy piecrusts, cakes that didn't rise, loaves of bread with a "core" in the center, biscuits that were gummy instead of flaky, and more, the don't-preheat dictum was modified—the word now was that it was unnecessary to preheat for some foods.

True. Ovens do not need to be preheated for casseroles, roasts, or any other foods that *(a)* are unleavened, or *(b)* do not have to begin browning as soon as they go in the oven. However, a little sensible observation led us to realize that many of these foods required a longer cooking time in an oven that was not preheated—in some cases, considerably longer than it would have taken to preheat the oven, because an oven with a large amount of cold food in it takes much longer to reach the required temperature than does an empty oven. The whole business turned out to be another teapot tempest. But there are still some diehards around who will say that preheating is not energy efficient. I have now supplied you with ammunition with which to refute them.

Finishing Touches

When you are through typing recipes, read them carefully to make certain that all elements are not only in place but also in the right place. Ideally, ask someone else—someone who can cook—to read the recipes as well; a fresh eye can often spot troubles you have overlooked or never even thought of. Make necessary corrections neatly, in ink.

Make certain that every word, paying particular attention to foreign words, is properly spelled, that grammar and punctuation are up to snuff. Check to see that necessary diacritical marks are in place; because many of these do not occur as characters on the average typewriter, put them in neatly by hand, in ink. And if, after all this, the recipe looks like a survivor of fire and flood, retype it. It's worth the trouble. Many an editor, looking at a sloppy, hard-to-read manuscript, has thought: "If this writer doesn't care enough to be neat, he doesn't care enough to have the manuscript published. Send it back!"

Chapter Four
Old-Pro Techniques: Writing Nonrecipe Material

Do your participles dangle, your infinitives split, your cases become entangled? Do your adjectives somehow end up modifying verbs and your adverbs cosy up to nouns? Would you fail to recognize a gerund if one came up and spat in your eye? Are you a modern-day Mrs. Malaprop or Dr. Spooner without even knowing it? Do you confuse like/as, imply/infer, parameter/perimeter, militate/mitigate, and all those other sets of words that pair up to trap the grammatically unwary?

If echo answers "yes," you are not really a writer.

"But," you protest, blushing and shuffling your feet, "this is only a cookbook, not the Great American Novel, for heaven's sake!"

Nonsense. There is no such thing as "only" writing, just as there is no such thing as "only a housewife." Everything committed to paper, from a note to the milkman to an erudite historical trilogy, should meet the accepted standards of grammar, punctuation, spelling, syntax, and vocabulary. As for the Great American Novel, it might be possible to pass off sloppy writing there as "the author's fascinatingly eccentric style," but in a cookbook, no way.

If, since you decided to write a cookbook, you've thought of it only in terms of recipes, it may come as something of a shock to be reminded that such a book harbors many other sorts of information between its covers. And all of that information, as well as the recipes, is the responsibility of the author. You. It is known to cookbookers as "peripheral material"—peripheral to the central information of the book, the recipes—but don't let that adjective fool you into thinking such material unimportant. It should be approached as thoughtfully, researched as thoroughly, presented as carefully as the recipes.

Unfortunately, the English language is trampled on, bent out of shape, ravished, and otherwise abused by many people who ought to—and, as a matter of fact, do—know better. "I was in a hurry," "I guess I was careless," or "It doesn't matter in this context" are the usual excuses offered, but they don't excuse. People in the writing business live by words, and ought to have sense enough to treat their livelihood with respect.

Just the other day, I was reading through a publisher's contract when one of those right/wrong pairs of words caught my eye. The phrase read: "These rights shall insure to the benefit of the author." Okay, fellas, whatever happened to *inure*? Has the creeping rot got you, too? Did a typist—I hope—simply make a typing error, or is the contract department unable to differentiate between inure/insure and did whoever proofread the contract fail to catch it?

Allowed to sink my teeth into the subject of sloppy writing, I could chew on it forever. But now that you've sworn not to let your ability to fight your way through pate/pâte/pâté be the alpha and omega of your cookbook writing skills, end of lecture and a return to cookbookery.

A BAGFUL OF BITS AND PIECES

Although there are many kinds of nonrecipe information that can legitimately be included in a cookbook, only a few are essential. They are:

A general introduction

Section introductions (with appropriate titles)

Captions (if there are illustrations)

An index

With the exception of the index, a cookbook lacking any of these could be at least marginally useful. However, without an overall introduction and a lesser one for each section, your book will seem cold and lacking in grace. No illustration should ever appear—in any book, not just a cookbook—without an identifying caption, no matter how self-evident the content of the illustration may seem to the author and editors; the only exception is a small line drawing or a meaningless but decorative squiggle—called a "spacer"—used to fill too-short pages. As for an index, any cookbook without one is a disaster.

The *general introduction* should entice the reader into the book, explain the book's reason for being, tell the reader why this book is different from others, what can be found in it that can't be found elsewhere. If you have theories on the art of cooking, this is the place to air them. If you have strong beliefs about nutrition, this is the place to enunciate them. But don't ramble and don't haul in extraneous material by the heels.

Unless what you have to say has definite, direct bearing on the body of the book that follows, don't say it. An introduction that wanders on, page after page after page, can be extremely off-putting.

Section titles and introductions should alert the reader to what's coming, signal anyone flipping through the book that a particular section is just what he or she is looking for. So again, as with a book title, don't call a section something cute but incomprehensible. When you title a section on bread, call it flat-footedly "Bread and Rolls," or lyrically "The Marvelous Aroma of Baking Bread," but not "That Magic Little Organism." Some readers may not know that yeast is a living organism (some of them, indeed, would be happier not knowing).

Each section introduction should enlarge on its title in telling the reader what lies ahead. Here, too, is the place to explain any cooking techniques common to all, or most, of the recipes in the section. Continuing the example of a section on bread, the introduction might explain the differences among pastry, bread, and all-purpose flour; what gluten is and its effect on the dough; why a loaf made with all rye or all whole-wheat flour will have a texture quite different from one made with all white flour; how to knead; what resting the dough accomplishes; the knocking technique for telling when a loaf of bread is done; why sugar helps yeast to rise; how to form a loaf—any or all of the dozens of facets of the art of bread-making.

Captions may be long and explanatory or very brief, depending on how the book is designed. Until it has been designed, you will not be required to supply captions, but bear them in mind because sooner or later they'll have to be written. If the design of the book does not allow for captions, set up an immediate howl.

The simplest caption is the unadorned title of the recipe the picture illustrates, such as "Nectar Cake With English Custard." A fuller caption could read, "A light dessert with the delightful flavor of burnt sugar, Nectar Cake is given a finishing touch with a spoonful of English Custard." In other words, long or short, a caption must identify what's in the picture. If the recipe does not appear on the same page as the picture or on the opposite page, the reader should be told where to find it, as in "Nectar Cake With English Custard, page 97." If you write captions before the book is cast—that is, before what material will appear on each page is determined—you will have to give an open page number, as "page 00." Later, you or an editorial person will go through and supply the missing page numbers; this is known as "satisfying folios." If you have ever seen a printed book—and who hasn't—with the "page 00" still there, where a number should be, it means that the satisfying has not been very satisfactory. Am I telling you more than you care to know? Not really. That is just one of the many things a book provides to worry about. A book should be worried about. From the tiniest pamphlet to the weightiest tome, a book is worth worrying about or it's not worth writing.

The *index* is an essential guide to what's in the book. Perhaps the first time around, a reader will go through the body of the book page by page, thinking, "That sounds good," or "I'll try that," or "Joe probably wouldn't like that." It is after that first perusal that an index comes into its own, because one of the key rules governing cookbooks is: Readers never, *never* remember the names of recipes, no matter how simple or complicated, how clumpish or far-out the names may be. Even if you've called your scrambled eggs Scrambled Eggs, don't count on anyone's remembering it. That's why a by-title index is hardly more useful than no index at all.

In a good, useful index, recipes should be categorized,

besides by title, by chief ingredient (beef, cheese, eggs, etc.), and by place in the meal (appetizers, main dishes, salads, etc.), at a bare minimum. If there is room—and there ought to be—main categories should be broken down; for example, desserts could be categorized as pies and pastry, cakes, cookies, puddings, chilled desserts, frozen desserts; meats at the least into beef, pork, lamb, veal, variety meats, poultry, fish and shellfish, and better still into roasts, stews, casseroles, creamed dishes, sautéed dishes, deep-fried foods as well. If there are quick/easy dishes in the book, there should be a quick/easy category in the index. Ditto low-calorie dishes, ditto make-ahead dishes, ditto party foods. If a category such as soups can be broken down into appetizer soups, main-dish soups, cold soups, and so on, so much the better. If cakes can be divided as butter, foam, chiffon, fruit, as well as layer, tube-pan, sheet, cupcakes, and petits fours, the index is thereby improved. By now, you get the idea.

Who prepares—makes, as it is called—the index? If you're lucky, some gloriously picky soul who has set him- or herself up in business as a professional indexer. There are many such freelancers, and very large publishing houses sometimes have an indexer-in-residence, sitting there on the premises, categorizing things from morn till dark, from year's beginning to year's end, amen. Don't feel sorry for them; they love it. However, by terms of your contract, it may fall to you, the author, to make the index. If so, you have two ways to go: Make the index yourself or hire a professional. Unless you've done it before, or are by nature a devout nit-picker, you're better off hiring someone—but be warned, they don't come cheap. One other alternative: An in-house indexer may make your index and his or her time be charged against royalties due you.

If you decide to be a do-it-yourself indexer, start early. As you type your tested recipes for the final manuscript, make out a file card for each, carrying the recipe title and a note about the chief ingredient. Put these away—alphabetically for this first go-round—in a file box. After the manuscript is on its way, occupy yourself with card shuffling, making as many duplicates as necessary to categorize as explained above; segregate these duplicates by category. If, at some point along the line, the title of a recipe or a number of recipes is changed, make those changes at once on *every* file card pertaining to that recipe. Later on, when you are supplied with cast-off galleys or page proofs (I'll explain these presently), you can add the folio (page number) for each recipe, again on every file card for that recipe, and the index will be ready to alphabetize, type, and send off. Or you may be asked by the publishing house for a blank index, typed alphabetically and by category but without folios, ready for the editors to add the page numbers.

NICE, BUT NOT NECESSARY

There are stripped-for-action cookbooks, and then there are cookbooks clad in as many layers of camisoles and petticoats and assorted froufrou as any Victorian lady. It is easy to err in either direction, but often greatest acceptability—from publisher and reader alike—lies in steering a comfortable middle course. Put together a manuscript that contains interesting, useful, inventive recipes; surround those recipes with sufficient pertinent, lively, helpful peripheral material to enhance the recipes but not to upstage them, and you have the formula for a successful cookbook.

Almost anything pertaining to food—buying it, storing it, preparing it, cooking it, garnishing and decorating it, enhancing it (as with sauces, toppings, frostings), eating it—is fair game to use as peripheral material in a cookbook, as long as the material relates in some way to the recipes you're using and the type of cookbook you're producing. Here are some possibilities:

Ingredient information (all about butter, all about sugar, etc.)

Shelf life of canned goods

Optimum freezer storage times

Product information (in commercial cookbooks)

Using and caring for kitchen tools and utensils

Glossary of cooking terms

Reasons for cooking failures

Preparation techniques (creaming, beating, etc.)

Anecdotes pertinent to the main text

Mail-order sources for ingredients (including addresses, zip codes)

Table of nutritional values

Table of calorie counts

Table of equivalents and substitutions

Time-and-temperature charts for cooking meats

Information on cooking with wine, beer, liquor, liqueurs

That's only a beginning. I could go on and on—and have been known to do so, unless forcibly restrained. These bits and pieces of peripheral information can take any form from a few lines set off in some way from the main text to graphs/charts that occupy several pages. The kinds and amounts of peripheral information you use and how it is presented should be governed by the kind of cookbook you are writing. That is, don't plop down bits of exotic-food lore in the midst of a family-dinners cookbook, or a table of calorie counts in a cookbook made up solely of gloriously rich desserts. Once again, common sense.

What is there to say about these subjects that will intrigue, or at the least inform, the reader? Plenty. Suppose you decide to do "All About Butter." Areas you might cover include how butter is made, how it is graded (AA, A, and B, by the USDA) and what each grade indicates, nutritive value, how to buy and store (including freezing), varieties (salted, sweet, whipped, etc.), how to measure. Want more? Add information about butter substitutes. Still more? Include a few simple butter sauces such as *beurre noisette,* maître d'hôtel butter, etc. Even more? How to clarify, how to make and use beurre manié. See? It's a cinch.

There are a couple more pieces of optional material that may be included in a cookbook: foreword and preface. These, if they are used, go in the front of the book, before the first recipe section. A foreword is written by someone other than the author, is signed and dated by the person who writes it, and generally extols the virtues of the book and its author.

Unless the foreword writer is well known and also works in the food field, there's not much point; a nuclear physicist, no matter how famous, isn't a proper foreword writer for a cookbook—unless, possibly, she is so good a friend that she has brunched, lunched, and dined at the author's table many times and can speak with authority on her or his credentials as a dynamite cook. On the other hand, if Julia Child happens to be your best friend, she is the perfect person to contribute a foreword to your book.

A preface is written by the author. It differs from the general introduction in that it concerns the author rather than the book. In a preface the author may explain how all the recipes in the book are a legacy from Great-aunt Agatha and why Aunt Aggie has a claim to fame; or the preface may detail how the author learned to cook (if the "how" is unusual and entertaining)—in other words, anything that explains the author's relationship to the book if, indeed, the relationship needs explaining and is interesting enough to be worth talking about. Otherwise, skip it and content yourself with an introduction.

CALL ME BY MY RIGHTFUL NAME

Pause here a moment and add a few more terms to your publishing vocabulary. The introduction as well as the foreword and/or preface, if any, are parts of the *front matter.* Also going to make up the front matter are the *title page,* a *recto* (right-hand) page on which appears the book's title, the author's name (and sometimes the name of the illustrator), and the publisher's name and city/state address; the *verso* (back side) of the title page carries the copyright notice and may also carry credit to the illustrator if it has not appeared on the title page, as well as credit to such people as, for example, a store that has loaned china to the author to be used as props in pictures; *half-title pages* (none, or one, but no more than two), which carry only the title of the book and are always recto pages. The *contents page,* always recto but which may be continued to the following verso page if it is long, carries a listing of everything in the book that follows the contents page—items such as foreword or preface, which may fall before the contents page, are usually not listed.

Acknowledgments, if used, may fall on a recto or verso page and should (very briefly, please) thank such people as an editor, a recipe tester, or someone or several someones who were of substantial assistance—"without whom this book could not have been written," as the saying goes, and I wish it wouldn't. Control yourself; don't thank the typewriter repair man who came so promptly to fix the *b* that was sticking, or your mother, who looked over your shoulder as you were typing page 78 and pointed out, "Goodness, *i* before *e* except after *c,* dear!"

A *dedication,* if you want to include one, should also be brief and restrained, not sloppily sentimental; it can be positioned on a recto or verso page. Front matter either does not carry folios (page numbers, remember?) or may be folioed in lowercase roman numerals, although the latter system is usually reserved for weightier tomes than cookbooks. In any case, material that falls before the contents page (title, half title, etc.) is not folioed.

The book's *back matter,* which is folioed, consists of whatever falls after the last page of the last section of the book, and may be made up of some of the peripheral material—glossaries, sources for ingredients, bibliography, and appendixes are suitable back-matter material—plus the index, or may consist solely of the index. (Incidentally, bear in mind that all right-hand pages carry odd numbers, all left-hand pages are even numbered.) Between the front matter and the back matter lies the meat of the project, the *body of the book.*

IT AIN'T WHAT YOU DO, IT'S THE WAY THAT YOU DO IT

The style in which you couch all the nonrecipe material in your cookbook should be governed by the audience to whom the book is addressed. If you're doing a children's cookbook, keep the text simple, light, and brief. Cookbooks composed of quick/easy recipes should not be burdened with long, rambling text, no matter how interesting; those who seek to get in and out of the kitchen in no time flat are unlikely to want to read about food at any length. In putting together an ethnic cookbook, keep strictly to yourself any ethnic jokes you might be tempted to include, and hold firmly in check your desire to lapse into dialect.

In a cookbook for adults who can be expected to be reasonably well acquainted with a kitchen and its contents, you have more leeway in producing nonrecipe text. But you still need to exercise intelligent self-control. Don't let the heady pleasure of putting words on paper lead you into wandering far from the subject, into dragging in anecdotes that, charming though they may be, have nothing to do with the subject at hand. Learn to trample on your baser impulses: If, for example, you tend to lard your everyday speech with foreign words and phrases, refrain when you're writing cookbook text. Take my word for it, "To each his own, right?" is far superior to "*Chacun à son goût, n'est-ce pas?*" in this context.

Whether your writing style is playful or austere, expansive or stingy, as long as it is your style you'll get along fine. Nonfiction, particularly nonfiction of this nuts-and-bolts kind, is no place to assume a new personality. It is unlikely to fit you any better than a cheap suit and, like such an unwise choice of clothing, may well rip at the seams and show the real you lurking beneath. An easy, be-yourself style is what you should aim for; you'll be comfortable with it, and so will your readers.

PLAY IT AGAIN, SAM

Unless you are blessed with such writing and typing talents as are seldom seen among mortals, your manuscript—both the recipe and the nonrecipe material—will certainly need some editing, probably some spot revising, possibly a total rewrite.

There are a great many different approaches to writing. Some writers scribble a brief outline, understandable to no one but themselves, and then start to write. Others make outlines so long and detailed that they feel as if they had already written the book before they actually begin. Some, unhampered by even the ghost of an idea, sit down at their typewriters, poise their hands above the keys, and wait for heaven to belt them with a thunderbolt of inspiration. Some revise and polish as they go, some blitz through a first draft and tidy up later.

My own approach is to make one of those loose, not-much outlines and then start putting words together into sentences, sentences into paragraphs while I'm doing something else, such as taking a shower, falling asleep, washing dishes, cooking. Although this sometimes leads to lapses such as forgetting to shampoo my hair while I'm under the shower, or adding the milk twice but the flour not at all as I make a cake, it does assure me of an even, orderly, satisfying flow of words when at last I sit down to write. If I am bored with a project, I trick myself into forging ahead, like people who set their watches ten minutes fast to make certain they won't be late. When I'm writing fiction, I stop for the day in the midst of an exciting scene so I'll be eager to return and finish it. I never quit at the end of a chapter or section, but always start the next, even if by only a couple of sentences, before I cover my typewriter for the day.

For some, the problem lies not so much in how to write as when. Unless you are blessed with inherited wealth and a covey of minions to do your bidding, all your time is unlikely to be your own. You doubtless have a house to keep, probably children as well, a husband or wife coming home hungry at the end of the day. You may have a full- or part-time job. There may be volunteer work that is important to you, an aerobics class that you enjoy, a sport that takes a good deal of your time, church work that is a pleasant obligation. When do you write? How do you manage to sandwich writing among all those other activities? Oddly enough, if you really want to, you do.

I remember talking, years ago, to a man who is now a very successful, very wealthy motion pictures writer-director. "Do you have trouble finding time to write?" I asked him.

"Do you?"

"Yes. There are so many other demands on my time, there's not enough of me to go around."

He shook his head. "Nonsense," he told me loftily. "If you really want to write, you will find time for it. If you really want to write, nothing else is half so important. Get up early. Stay up late. Force the day to yield more hours than it has. Make writing your first priority, and assign lesser places to everything else."

I glared at him resentfully. Easy for him to talk! He did have a nine-to-five editorial job, but he also had a wife who coped with everything else. When he went home at the end of the day, he kissed his wife, played for exactly fifteen minutes with his children, ate his ready-when-you-are dinner, and the remainder of the evening was all his. Ditto all day Saturday and Sunday.

On the other hand, I worked full-time at a radio station, went to night school twice a week, modeled hats and gloves and shoes (the rest of me didn't come up to modeling standards) whenever I could get jobs, ran open auditions for the radio station, emceed fashion shows on an average of twice a month, worked as an actress in radio dramas and little theater, shopped and cooked, and kept my apartment passably clean. All that seemed to leave little time for the activities I enjoyed, horseback riding and dancing and swimming, let alone writing. But I could, I decided, reorganize a bit. Much as I loved riding, it was not necessary to heave myself out of bed and onto the back of a horse every morning of the week. My very small apartment didn't need much housekeeping, even of my once-over-lightly sort. I could, as I'd had to when I lived at home under my conservative mother's vigilant eyes, confine my dating to weekends. With a bit of maneuvering, I could dump those auditions on someone else's shoulders. I wanted to keep the radio acting, but I could give up stage appearances; after all, at six feet tall without heels, I had to do comedy or characters; ingenue and leading-lady roles were out because, particularly in those days, juveniles and leading men—forgetting the few Gary Coopers and James Stewarts—stood at most five-eight. All of a sudden, there was time to write after all.

Because I am a night person, I wrote in the evenings and as far into the night as I could. But if you are a day person, get up early, before the rest of the house is stirring. If you have children, return to your writing when they are at school or while young ones nap. Give up unnecessary things, such as kaffeeklatsches, soap operas, and excursions to the local shopping mall "just to look around." No matter how dedicated a homemaker you are, it is not necessary to keep your house as if you expected the Good Housekeeping Institute to spring a surprise inspection at any moment. Cook for two meals at once: braised lamb shoulder one night, lamb curry later; pot roast of beef one night, beef salad later; roast chicken one night, chicken pot pie later. If you bake, go on a baking binge one day a week—a cake, a pie, a batch of cookies, two loaves of bread, a pan of cinnamon rolls—and forget it the rest of the time. Shop once a week, list in hand and the kids, if at all possible, elsewhere. Entertain as simply as possible, at brunches and buffets (serving those tested-recipe foods you've stored in your freezer) rather than sit-down meals. All at once you, too, will have time to write if you really want to. And if you've tagged along with me up to this point, you'll have a cookbook manuscript—recipes plus peripheral material—ready.

And now that you have it, what do you do with it?

Chapter Five
Assault on the Citadel: Selling Your Book

Who publishes cookbooks? Publishing houses, of course. There are many of those, and many kinds—from big to small, from generalists to specialists. There are package houses, as well—which in one sense are publishing houses (and often call themselves that), although their function may be very far removed from that of a "real" publisher. Sometimes, although quite rarely, printers are also publishers. Finally, individuals—single persons, two or three collaborators, a large or small committee, or even a giant corporation or conglomerate not normally concerned with cookbooks or books of any sort—may act as a publisher for one or several books.

What motivates every one of these ill-assorted people? The twin desires that lie behind all onward-and-upward endeavors: fame and fortune.

MET ANY GOOD PUBLISHERS LATELY?

Like the rest of us, publishers come in all shapes and sizes, and are blessed with—or suffer from—a broad range of reputations. Some publishing houses are very small, are staffed by a very few people, and put out two, three, four books a year.

Some are huge, with large, departmentalized staffs, and annually put out books by the several hundreds. More often than not, the very small houses publish whatever has taken the editor's fancy and the hell with categories. The very big houses are usually the generalists, publishing fiction from glorious to gruesome, and embracing such categories as romances, straight novels, humor, mysteries, science fiction; nonfiction in the form of biography, history, politics, science (including mathematics, physics, and medicine among others), as well as other stern-visage subjects, including cookbooks; religion-oriented books; books for children, juveniles, and teens, often lumped together as "young readers"; textbooks—elementary, secondary, and college; how-to books, offering instructions on how to do anything that might ever occur to anybody under any circumstances (plant gardens, lose weight, be beautiful, build a log cabin, whatever); nonbooks, covering everything that doesn't fit neatly into any other category, including dirty jokes (clean ones, too, but they don't sell nearly as well), cartoons, collections of lists, humor of various sorts, with titles such as *Teaching Your Shih Tzu to Play the Glockenspiel* or *Frontal Lobotomy Made Easy,* patterns for needlework and crafts, and many others, including that pinnacle of the nonbook category, the handsome, beautifully bound book full of blank pages on which the reader is invited to inscribe his or her own deathless prose.

Have I forgotten anything? Sure I have. Poetry. Poetry is publishing's orphan child. Most publishing houses feel that they ought to publish poetry—after all, it's so classy!—but are restrained by the fact that poetry does not sell other than to the poet's parents and Uncle Julius. Once in a great while an abysmally awful versifier comes along, a publisher takes a chance, and to everyone's chagrin (except the poet's, of course) the book sells like crazy. But if it's good poetry, forget it, unless the publishing house wishes to take a loss while at the same time enhancing its reputation.

About the only thing all publishers have in common is that they put out books. From there, they go off in all directions. Some—a large number—are top-heavy, with too many chiefs and not enough indians; some few are bottom-heavy, with the editors working their butts off and the other ranks polishing their nails and setting up assignations for Saturday night. Some editorial departments are housed in pleasant, airy, roomy offices; others are packed ten-deep into dungeons.

I remember well the now-dead editor-in-chief of a big, prestigious publishing house, whose office was as long and narrow as a boxcar, with the light at the end of the tunnel provided by a single slit of a window; this wise and witty man spent all his days and many of his nights surrounded by piles of manuscripts, served by a shrew of a secretary and a totally inadequate staff. In the same era, in an equally big, prestigious house, an editor-in-chief who was one of the world's true jerks presided over his huge staff of cretins from a large, handsome, corner office suitably decorated with a glorious Persian carpet, a Corot on one wall, and French antiques all over the place.

A game of musical chairs is in constant progress, with editors and sub-editors bounding from publishing house to publishing house with reckless abandon, seeking perfection that, not surprisingly, never materializes. What are they looking for? Pleasanter working conditions, some of them. A boss they can relate to in one way or another. Better pay (no matter what you may have heard or dreamed of, editorial people as a class are overworked and underpaid). In some cases, a better—or, at least, different—class of book on which to work.

EDITORIAL HIERARCHY

Trade Book Department—Fiction and Nonfiction

Publisher

Editor-in-Chief

Art Director	Production Manager	Rights and Permissions	Managing Editor	Acquisitions Editor	Senior Editor
Designers	Assistant	Assistant	Copy Editor	Associate Editor	
			Proofreader	Assistant Editor	
			Indexer	Editorial Assistant	
				Clerk-Typist	

In a small publishing house, one person may serve in several of these capacities; in a very large publishing house, there may be a number of acquisitions and senior editors, and multiple associates and assistants, as well as one or several secretaries and perhaps a typing pool. Freelance copy editors, proofreaders, and indexers are often hired as needed, to work short-term. Expert readers to "vet" manuscripts are almost always freelancers. Books with a potential for libel, plagiarism, or right-to-privacy suits go outside the editorial purview to an in-house or out-of-house lawyer versed in publishing law.

Large publishing houses may also have one or more imprints (recognize them by the line "A Letitia Abigail Witherspoon Book"), semiautonomous small publishers working under the wing of the big one; each of these will usually have an abbreviated staff. There will be other editorial departments, too—religious, textbook, juvenile, etc.—each with its own editor and staff. And if the publisher puts out paperbacks, there will be a separate, complete staff for that operation.

Not strictly editorial (in the sense of the structuring of

words into books), but essential to the editorial scheme of things, is the art department, responsible for the physical appearance of the books. It is headed by an art director, supported by a staff that may include designers, type specialists, lettering specialists, and mechanical makers. Freelance designers may be hired as well, and freelance artists will certainly be.

There are many noneditorial positions in a publishing house: the sales manager and his staff of traveling salesmen; the comptroller and his staff of accountants and bookkeepers; secretaries and perhaps a typing pool for the business side of the operation; "front people" such as receptionists and telephone operators; people to fill both mail orders and those sent in by the book salesmen; people who physically handle shipments of books (warehouses, where books are held, are generally in some place other than the building that houses editorial personnel); and, depending on the individual publishing house, various other departments.

Small publishing houses cope with the same functions on a double-in-brass basis, the assistant editor finding him- or herself running the switchboard at lunch time, the editor-in-chief reading proof in emergencies, and so on. Somehow, it all gets done.

And there are all the semifrivolous reasons, such as a location nearer home, or the fact that the previous house had no eligible males or females in the editorial department, or a general working policy less rigid than the one that required you to turn in the old stub before you could have a new pencil.

While I'm on the subject, let me tell you something about editors. Believe me, having been at various points in my career an editor and an author and at a few schizoid times both at once, I am in a position to know. Editors are human. They have headaches, are allergic to poison ivy, have high-to-low/low-to-high mood swings. They can be right, but they can also be wrong. They have anxiety attacks and temper tantrums, spells of depression and fits of euphoria. They have burdensome mortgages, wives/husbands who do not understand them, sick children, interfering mothers. In other words, they have their ups and downs, their good days and their bad days, just like everyone else. Fortunately, with a few notable exceptions, they are highly intelligent people, which can make up for a whole collection of faults.

WHO DOES WHAT TO WHOM

Just as there is no point in submitting a novel to a publishing house that puts out only nonfiction, there is no point in sending a cookbook to a house to which cookbooks are anathema. How do you find out? You make a survey.

First, keep in mind that *general publishers* put out books in all, or at the least many, categories. *Specialty publishers* concentrate on one kind of book, as broad a classification as only fiction or only nonfiction, or as narrow as only parapsychology or only buns-and-guns thrillers; some, happily, publish only—or mostly—cookbooks, but these are few. *Package houses* prepare books (in many or few categories, depending on the individual house) for other publishers; they may do as little as contracting with the author and carrying through the various stages of manuscript preparation, or as much as printing and binding the book and delivering it, ready to ship, to the primary publisher. *Vanity presses* function in the same manner as general or specialty publishers, with one very important exception: Here the total cost, or the major portion of the cost, of producing and selling the book is underwritten by the author; the press supplies only expertise, in horrendously varying degrees.

What about *self-publishing* (which is not, no matter what you have heard, the same as vanity publishing)? That is a whole other ballgame, far removed from publishing houses—so far removed that we'll treat it as a separate subject, beginning on page 185.

Besides needing to know what kinds of books a publisher puts out, it helps to learn how many. A house that puts out books by the hundreds each year has a certain amount of turn-around room in which to operate; a house whose annual output is under ten books can be very choosy indeed (that they sometimes choose to put out some real bummers isn't the point here).

How, if you are not in the publishing business, can you find out what houses publish what categories and how many books overall? By consulting other books, put out by other publishers for this very purpose.

There is one big publisher-for-publishers, R. R. Bowker Company, and several publishers-for-writers, such as Writer's Digest Books and *The Writer.* All these annually put out reference books very useful to writers. Bowker's *Books in Print* lists all the books that their publishers have not declared out of print (no longer to be published) at the time the lists are compiled; in the latest volume, that amounts to 619,000 titles in print. Of that very large number, 80 percent of the titles were put out by only three percent of the 15,000 active publishers. Bowker also publishes *Paperback Books in Print;* 69

percent of those 15,000 active publishers have paperback books in print, representing 37 percent of all in-print books. The third of Bowker's big annual book directories is one more useful to authors seeking a home for their brain children: *Subject Guide to Books in Print.* There you can find the title, author, and publisher of every book in print in any category, including the one you're looking for, cookbooks. All of these hardcover directories are huge, awkward to use, and exceedingly expensive, but they are put out primarily for publishers, bookstores, and libraries. Consult them at your local library, and if your eyesight isn't all it might be, make sure to bring your glasses.

Most useful of all to writers is another of Bowker's annuals, *Literary Market Place,* known affectionately in the trade as *LMP.* This is an oversize paperback of (currently) 23 pages of front matter, 520 pages of body, and 237 of appendix, into which is packed an amount of information you won't believe until you begin to browse. Consider only one of the fourteen major categories listed on the contents page: Book Publishing. Under that heading you can locate book publishers of the United States, listed alphabetically (along with their addresses, the kinds and numbers of books published in the past year, names of company officers and editors, date the company was founded, and other tidbits of information); next, these publishers are repeated, but this time classified by geographic location; next, the publishers are repeated yet again, classified by fields of activity (such categories as Fine Editions, Directories, Scholarly Books, and so on); finally, the publishers are classified by subject matter (Agriculture, Behavioral Sciences, Drama, and so on, through seventy-some subject-matter classifications, including Cookbooks, Food, Beverages).

Beyond the book publishing information, *LMP* contains a treasure-house of other, related data. Here's a random sampling: book clubs, literary contests and grants, book review syndicates, literary agents, TV programs featuring books, magazine and newspaper publishers—and this list barely scratches the surface. Finally, at the end, in *LMP*'s yellow pages, is the Names & Numbers section, which used to be put out as a separate volume; this is the telephone directory of the publishing business, giving company and individual names listed alphabetically. This is not particularly useful to writers who have no connections in the publishing business, but could come in handy if you want to locate that nice editor from Snodgrass Books, whom you met at a writers' conference but who is no longer listed under Snodgrass in the book publishers' section.

Does all this sound as if no other type of reference could possibly be needed by a writer looking for a place to sell a book? Not quite true. The directories (such as *Writer's Market, Fiction Marketplace,* etc.) published each year by Writer's Digest Books and The Writer can sometimes give you a bit of information that you can't find in *LMP.* How does this happen? To begin with, book publishing houses, large and small and in-between, are not the best-organized businesses in the world. There is a certain amount of regimentation (I once worked in a publishing office where every morning at eleven a whistle blew and everybody pell-melled up to the roof to do calisthenics), but a place for everything and everything in its place, as well as a person for everything and every person doing his thing, is not the guiding precept of most publishers.

In a big publishing house, a request for information from Bowker or one of the others will probably be routed to a person whose business it is to take care of such things, and he or she will fill out the form, guided by a loosely defined policy covering such matters ("Don't list me in *LMP* this time. I'm sick to death of fielding telephone calls that ought to go to Joe!"), and mail it back. It is entirely possible, however, that the filler-outer may have come down with Lassa fever, and the beleaguered soul told off to do his/her work may note the deadline, fill out the form without any knowledge of policy on the matter, and send it back. In small houses, there generally is no policy, and the person least busy at the moment will fill out and return the form; sometimes Tight-lip Lucy, whose own policy is secrecy at all costs, will fill out one form, while Loose-lip Larry, the company gossip, will fill out another. In such a case, Lucy's form will tell the company name and address and that's about all, while Larry's will tell everything, including the maiden name of the bookkeeper's third wife. It does, indeed, pay to compare one book's listing with another's.

THE GAME'S AFOOT!

When your manuscript of a first book is finished, or at least so well along that you know definitely where you're going and how you're getting there, it's time to research publishers. Arm yourself with notebook and pen (and those glasses, if you need them) and set out on your quest.

1. Go first to a bookstore—or two or three—and browse in the cookbooks section. Make note of the titles and publishers of books that are particularly attractive, as well as

those that resemble in some way the book you are working on and the publishers who have more than two cookbooks in the section.

2. Next, go to the library—the main one downtown—and repeat the browsing and note-making routine in the cookbooks section.

3. Remove yourself to the general reference section. Consult *Subject Guide to Books in Print* and either photocopy or, if this is not allowed, copy by hand the names of the publishers under the Cookbooks heading. Consult *Literary Market Place,* and copy the publishers listed in *LMP*'s Cookbooks section. Compare the two lists: If publishers appear on one but not the other, look those up in *LMP*'s by-alphabet listing of publishers to see if you can find out why—the dropout may simply be an oversight on one list, or it may be that the publisher put out only one cookbook and therefore hardly qualifies as a publisher in that category.

4. Look up, in the Book Publishers section of *LMP,* all the publishing houses on both lists, and read carefully all the information printed under each heading. You'll learn at the very least where the publishing house is located, how long it has been in business, and how many books it put out in the previous year. You will also learn what kinds of books it publishes; sure, it's on the cookbook publishers list, but one cookbook and forty-three college texts indicates something of an imbalance, while eighteen cookbooks is cause for celebration. You'll also learn the name of the person to whom cookbook queries should be addressed—and the type(s) of query accept-

able—or, if not, the name of the nonfiction editor or of the editor-in-chief. (If only the names of the business-type officers of the company are listed, search elsewhere; you'd be astounded to learn how totally uninterested in books of any description the presidents of some book publishing houses can be.)

5. Make a new list of the publishers that seem to you to be most interesting/promising, along with the pertinent information you've learned about each. Cross-check this with listings for each of these publishers in several other publishing directories, such as Writer's Digest Books' *Writer's Market.* You may learn nothing new about some, but you may learn a great deal about others. Add anything you learn to your new list.

Okay, you're in business. Trot the list home, sit down, put your feet up, and do an in-depth study of what you've learned and what you can deduce from what you've learned. Number the publishers in order of their appeal to you, then type up a nice, clean, order-of-preference list.

"YOU DON'T HAPPEN TO WANT A GOOD COOKBOOK, DO YOU?"

Queries rank right up there with sympathy notes as among the more difficult writing chores. This is delicate ground. You don't want to toot your own horn so loudly it breaks the editor's eardrums, but on the other hand, hanging your head and muttering will get you nowhere.

To begin with, follow the leads you've gleaned from your research. If the publishing house you're addressing says it will read no unsolicited manuscripts, but only queries, a preliminary letter is called for. If it asks for query and synopsis or outline, that is what you must send; if query, outline, and sample text are required, send all three. If the publishing house wants a full manuscript, go back and read that part again to make certain; few publishers are willing to look at unsolicited nonfiction manuscripts, even if a complete fiction manuscript is requested. (Convention among publishers holds that fiction writers are more temperamental and thus less reliable than those who write nonfiction, and the thinking is that although chapters one and two may be great, chapters three through seventeen can well be duds.)

If you have been following me politely, you already have a working title, a rough outline, and good section titles. A list of those section titles, plus a brief description of the material in that section under each title, is the simplest kind of cookbook outline, and is always acceptable. If a portion of the text is asked for, send the general introduction, one section introduction, and four to six of the best—most unusual, most interesting, most delicious-sounding—recipes. Tidy all this up, type clean copies, and read the copies carefully.

Now you are cornered. There is nothing left to do but write that query letter. Here are the points to cover:

1. Address the proper editor.

2. Say that you are offering a cookbook (the editor probably handles several other categories of nonfiction books as well) for consideration, and describe the contents briefly—what category of cookbook yours falls into, how you came to write it (but only if the reason is interesting), where the recipes come from (but only if their origin is interesting).

3. State your credentials: tell the editor what qualifies you to write this book. If you have written other cookbooks, name them and their publishers. If you have written food-related articles, cite them and the publication(s) in which they appeared. If you have had anything to do with food—been a cook, worked for a caterer, worked for a food processor or manufacturer, helped put out a community fund-raiser cookbook, even been chairman of the monthly parish dinner at your church—say so. If you have no credentials other than long experience as the family cook/homemaker, state that—it's experience not to be sneezed at.

4. If you are not submitting an outline, give the editor some idea of the size of the book by stating the number of sections and an average of the number of recipes per section. On the other hand, if you are submitting an outline, say so; if you are submitting sample recipes, say so. But do not, in either case, describe them in elaborate detail—the editor is able to read.

5. Remember that this is neither an obituary nor an announcement of the subject for your doctoral thesis, so don't be oversolemn. On the other hand, restrain yourself from being so cute that the editor is seized by a sudden fit of nausea. Neat but not gaudy is the way to go. Sound fresh and light. Be straightforward. Neither plod nor romp.

6. When you are finished, shut up.

Why that last direction? Some writers, especially those new to the game, have a horrid tendency to run on, because they know that when they have finished the query letter they're going to have to pack the whole business up and trot it to the post office—the action that they've been looking forward to for months but that, now the moment has arrived, they suddenly cannot bear to face.

A final observation: Be yourself. You wrote this book, and now you must stand behind it. You must be enthusiastic about it, or you wouldn't have embarked on the project in the first place. Let your enthusiasm show, because enthusiasm in you is likely to engender a similar response in the editor.

ONE, OR ONE OF MANY?

When I started out working in the publishing business, sending a query—or, worse, a manuscript—to more than one editor at a time was tantamount to being caught with your hand in the poor box. "No photocopies," instructions to writers admonished. That was because photocopying was in its infancy, and if you were able to read as much as half of any photocopied page, you considered yourself lucky. Times have changed, and so have copying machines. Today the copy can not only be read in its entirety but may, on the whole, be better looking than the original. And it is no longer a sin to make multiple submissions. However, be governed by what is told you by *LMP* or *Writer's Market* or other guides for writers. If the word is no photocopies, send the original. If the word is no multiple submissions, abide by it. Most publishing houses now accept photocopies. Not as many, but still a large number, have no objections to multiple submissions. Just make certain you stick to the rules of the particular publisher you are addressing.

A last rule: Don't forget the all-important SASE—self-addressed stamped envelope. Publishers are very tetchy on this subject, and no wonder, postal rates being what they are!

NOR ALL THY PIETY NOR WIT CAN BRING IT BACK . . .

If you are a first-book writer, the moment you irrevocably consign your manuscript to the post office or express company or whatever, you will want it back. All sorts of wonderful ideas for improving it by at least 500 percent will come crowding into your head. As in the General Confession, you will realize that you have "left undone those things we ought to have done, and done those things we ought not to have done, and there is no health in us." Forgotten recipes—the very best ones, of course—will mutely rebuke you. Clever turns of phrase that would have brightened your query will now leap to mind.

Forget it. What's done is done. Console yourself that first ideas are usually the best ideas, and go on about your business.

How will you know that the manuscript has arrived safely? You won't unless you use some delivery method that provides for a return receipt. Do not include with the manuscript a postcard to be mailed back to you by the person who takes in and opens your precious parcel. Do not telephone the publishing house, all a-flutter, to say you realize of course that they haven't had time to read the manuscript, and you certainly aren't trying to hurry them, no indeed, but you just want to make sure of its safe arrival. Do not write to the editor, close on the heels of having sent your manuscript, to make the same query. These are what sportswriters call "bush," meaning bush league, the lowest position on baseball's totem pole. In other words, amateurish. Tacky.

Now you wait. Grit your teeth, prepare to exhibit the patience of a saint and the fortitude of a martyr at whose vitals the lions are gnawing, and wait. Wait until you absolutely cannot wait another minute, and then wait twice as long.

How long? Although it may seem like forever and a day, the actual period will be anywhere from several weeks to several months. Generally speaking, a plain query will be answered fairly soon, a query plus samples in a somewhat longer time, and a full manuscript considerably longer. While you are waiting, console yourself with this: Rejections usually arrive sooner than acceptances.

Why does it take so unconscionably long for a publishing house to reply? In the first place, remember what I said before: In general, editorial departments are understaffed and overworked. In the second place, the top priority in any editorial office is to read, edit, design, copy-edit, and send to the typesetter those manuscripts already contracted for, the ones that, heaven willing, will appear as books in the next publishing season. Editing requires enormous amounts of time, often because manuscripts arrive in a sorry state, but sometimes simply because, by nature, editors cannot leave well enough—or even good enough—alone. They edit for the sake of improvement and/or they edit for the sake of editing.

I know, believe me. I never read a book without a pencil to hand; like a cat observing a mouse, I wait, breath held, to pounce on an infelicitous phrase, a bit of suspect punctuation, a misused word, a nasty typo, or—oh joy!—an error of fact. Never mind that the book is printed and between covers, far beyond calling back; never mind that both the author and the luckless editor may be long dead; never mind, even, that the book is a great one, inspired in conception, beautifully written, skillfully edited. Once an editor, always an editor. Seek out that misplaced comma, expunge that unfortunate simile, tote that barge, lift that bale!

So, the editors are busy editing. And what of the junior staff, the assistants and apprentices? They are up to their armpits in slush, and sinking fast. "Slush" is the term for unsolicited manuscripts, the ones that come in "over the transom," and that includes unsolicited queries as well. And what of the associate editors? They are reading manuscripts, too, the ones that once came to the publisher's attention as queries and were answered with a cautious "We would like to see an outline and two sample chapters of your book."

Besides their editing and reading, all the editorial people are answering phones that ring constantly. They are attending meetings. They are breaking in new staff members who arrived in response to the dingdong of publishing's musical chairs. They are writing letters. They are writing synopses and critiques of manuscripts they feel are worth passing along to the next-above editor in the pecking order. They are going out to lunch or taking a few minutes off to eat at their desks. In between, they are explaining to authors that no, they can't look through the 183-piece slush pile to see if a particular manuscript is there. Or they are listening to their spouses/housekeepers report that *(a)* the house is on fire, *(b)* the washer has overflowed again, or *(c)* Johnny has fallen out of the plum tree and broken his left femur. In spite of all this, sooner or later someone will get to your query, and better still, answer it. Patience and fortitude, remember?

THANKS, BUT NO THANKS

If the answer is yes, break out the champagne. If it is no—much more likely than yes, unfortunately—what do you do? You turn your material around and immediately send it to the next publisher on your list, pausing only to retype the query letter and to make certain that no one has jotted a telephone number on one of the margins or spilled morning coffee on page two of the outline. If it comes back from the second publisher, turn it around and send it to the third, and so on and on until at last you strike gold. Straighten your spine, during this process, and keep firmly in mind that such books as *Jonathan Livingston Seagull* and *Peyton Place,* to name only two of dozens of bestsellers, saw the inside of virtually every possible publishing house before they found someone willing to take a chance and give them a home. You say these are not good examples, one a fantasy—always difficult to sell—and the other hardly what could be called literature? All right, what about *Ironweed,* which won the 1983 Pulitzer Prize for fiction? It saw the offices of Random House, Holt, Dutton, Harper and Row, Knopf, Harcourt, Dial, Farrar Straus, Atheneum, Houghton Mifflin, and Avon, before Viking (on a second submission and pushed by one of their big-selling authors) decided to publish the book.

Books and the queries that are the ideas for books are rejected for a number of reasons. It is entirely possible that, being mortal and subject to mortal error, the editor hated your manuscript on sight. Or—and this is sometimes true and sometimes a let-'em-down-easy excuse—there may be something in the house, already purchased, that bears too close a resemblance to yours. Or the house may have contracted for all the cookbooks it is prepared to publish this season and the next, or may even have recently decided no longer to publish cookbooks at all. Or, face it, your book may simply not be good enough for that publishing house, not meet its standards.

Unfortunately, very seldom will you get any clue as to why the query was rejected. You will simply be told, politely, that your idea "does not suit any of our present publishing programs," or that "we are not accepting any unsolicited book ideas at the present time," or some other equally unfathomable excuse. Don't waste time in futile breast-beating. And don't telephone the publishing house to see if you can learn a more understandable reason for the rejection—you'll be humiliated to learn that no one remembers your brainchild. Simply enter in your records the name of the publishing house, the date the query was sent out, and the date it was returned, and try, try again.

SOMEONE TO WATCH OVER YOU

At some point in your writing career, you will say to yourself, "I ought to have an agent." The thoughtful answer to that is yes and no.

On the face of it, an agent looks like the promise of salvation to a harried, much-rejected writer. However, consider this: If you have no publishing track record and only a wad of rejection slips to show for your trouble, few successful agents are going to take you on, and an unsuccessful agent is worse than none. Once in a while a good agent will take on an absolute unknown, seeing something in a manuscript or idea that he is sure he can sell, but such happy accidents are rare —and in the field of cookbooks virtually nonexistent. Many agents feel that cookbooks aren't really writing at all. Indeed, many feel that way about all nonfiction. At any rate, unless your name is Beard or Child or the like, you're unlikely to find a good agent to take you on—and if your name is one of those, an agent is the last thing you need.

Understandably, whether or not to take on a new client is, to an agent, a matter of economics. The bottom line is usually $5,000: if you cannot generate that much, or more, in annual sales, the agent can't afford you. Can you afford an agent? Yes. The agent's bite out of each sale—10 percent, in some cases 15—is more than made up for by the fact that he takes all the aggravation off your shoulders, that he or she can usually negotiate a better price than you could for the same product, and that he or she can usually generate more sales in a given time than the nonagented writer can. But remember that all this is predicated on you—on your churning out a large body of good, salable work and accomplishing this rapidly and reliably. Obviously, the more good stuff you give an agent to sell, the harder that agent will work for you, because lining your pockets also lines his or hers.

If all that sounds to you like the sun coming up in a burst of glory, remember that for every sunrise there is a sunset. Before an agent can do all those lovely things for you, you have to make a connection with one, and a good agent, like a good man, is hard to find. Not that there aren't a great many agents available; the publishing world is crawling with them. But we're talking about a *good* agent. All the others are liabilities.

Wherever you live, unless possibly it's Snooker's Corners, population 187, there will be author's agents in your hometown. Such agents are more likely to be willing to work with you than New York agents are—New York is the throbbing heart of the publishing business—but they are, on the other hand, less likely to be useful. They don't have the at-hand contacts, the wide circle of friends in the business, the ease of sending a manuscript down the street instead of across the country, the ear to the ground that picks up signals about what's new, what's wanted, who has a gap in the spring list, who will throw up if one more cookbook comes in this month, who is about to lose his or her job, who is about to take a better one elsewhere. Once in a great while it's possible to luck into a New York agent who has retired to your town but is still shepherding several authors to keep his or her hand in; however, as few people leave the New York publishing scene other than with a gun at their heads, such agents are seldom to be found. Los Angeles is the only place other than New York where a large population of agents works, but most of these are interested only in film or TV material.

How can you tell whether a local agent can do you any good? You can't, with absolute certainty. But there are some signposts to guide you. Look in *LMP* and *Writer's Market* to see if the agent is listed and what information there is about him or her. Ask questions. What sales did the agent make last year and for how much? To what publishers? From what clients? Does he or she ever go to New York? How often? Is the agent a member of an organization of agents? (This doesn't guarantee respectability, but on the other hand, no such organization will take in an agent with a long record of gypping his clients.)

Tread carefully with agents who charge manuscript-reading fees. Some are perfectly reliable and respectable; some are in business for the sole purpose of reading manuscripts, sending them back with a regretful letter saying the material is not salable, and pocketing the fee. The score here is, unfortunately, heavily on the side of the unscrupulous.

How do publishing houses feel about agents? Some are very fond of them, a few even to the point of refusing to look at anything that does not arrive with an agent's blessing. Some put up with them, but without any love lost. Some resent them because they can, more often than not, get more for a manuscript than can the author who is selling him- or herself. Some consider them a rascally necessity.

OH, BEAUTEOUS DAY!

Whether you sell on your own or have an agent to do it for you, some lovely morning the mail person will ride up on a white charger, carrying on tip of lance a letter of acceptance rather than rejection.

Then what?

Chapter Six
A Consummation Devoutly To Be Wish'd: The Sold Book

On that lovely morning, when along with a couple of catalogs, a sheaf of bills, a notice congratulating you on being chosen one of the lucky ones allowed to buy an acre of Alaskan tundra for your very own, and a gossipy missive from your cousin in Hoboken, the mail carrier brings that all-important letter, try to take the event in stride.

Sure, you've had communications from publishers before, rather more of them than you care to think about. But this one is different. It is not thick, indicating the return of your query material. But neither is it overly thin, as a rejection slip or a brief "no, thanks" note is. It has some bulk, but neither too much nor too little. It fills the envelope top to bottom and side to side. It is, you discover when you can bring yourself to open it, a well-hedged, carefully worded letter of almost-acceptance. Stripped of its safeguards, the letter says in effect, "We like your proposal and the portions of manuscript you sent; we feel that we would like to publish this book, provided an agreement can be reached."

You pick yourself up off the floor, pour yourself a cup of coffee or something stronger if the sun is over the yardarm, sit down, and read the letter again. And again. Almost unbelievably, you have been promoted from aspiring writer to published author in one fell swoop. You are no longer a puttering amateur, but a competent professional. Hallelujah!

BETWEEN CUP AND LIP

After a while, you'll notice that the tone of the letter is restrained, even standoffish. What's the matter—aren't they as excited as you are? Well, no. Books are their business, and one more new book is hardly the cause for unconfined joy that it is to you. Besides, publishers know from long experience that there are a dozen things that can go wrong, and many of them will. They have, in their day, written to a writer saying that they wish to buy the proposed book—and never heard from the writer again. They have asked to see more of a manuscript that particularly caught their fancy—and in has come a mess of junk bearing no resemblance to the query material. They have asked to see more of a manuscript—and been told that the book has already been sold to someone else, although the author had made no previous indication that this was a simultaneous submission. They have made to an author what seemed to them a decent, if modest, offer—and been told to stuff it. (I once, in my innocence, made what seemed to me to be an attractive and reasonably substantial offer to an author and received in return a how-dare-you diatribe, couched in unprintable terms and ending with a threat to sue me.) If there is among authors—and, believe me, there *is*—a consensus that publishers are a bit peculiar, there is a parallel feeling among publishers that most writers are not playing with a full deck. There exists a large body of evidence supporting each side.

But right now, here you are with your (cautious) letter of acceptance clutched in your fist. Pause a moment to think about how that letter came into being. First, somebody reasonably far down on the publisher's totem pole—perhaps an assistant editor or a freelance reader—liked your proposal well enough to bump it up to someone with more authority—a senior editor or an acquisitions editor. He or she liked it too, well enough to speak to the editor-in-chief about it or to write that authority a report praising it; the manuscript was then scheduled for presentation at an editorial meeting in the near future. (Bear in mind that "near," in the publishing business, is a very elastic word.) Sooner or later, your manuscript appeared on the agenda of a pub meeting and was kicked around by those present: the editor-in-chief, perhaps a representative of the publisher, the managing editor, and a selection of editors with a certain amount of seniority and clout; present also may have been salespeople and production people.

When your manuscript was presented by the editor sponsoring it, someone surely said: "Oh, no! Not another cookbook!" Someone else: "That doesn't sound like such a hot idea." Someone else: "What makes this different from the three cookbooks we already have in the works?" Someone else: "All cookbooks are stolen—who'd the writer steal this one from?" Someone else: "We'd be lucky if the darned thing sold a hundred copies." Someone else: "What's the writer's name? Smith? I don't trust people named Smith." Someone else: "I don't know the writer, but I have a gut feeling we'll have trouble with this one." Someone else: "Let's not waste any more time on it."

You will have noticed by now that pub meetings bear a

horrid resemblance to sorority rush-week meetings. In spite of that, your book somehow survived the meeting, having been fought for tooth and nail by those who think it's a viable publishing project and who, by now, feel about it as one feels about an orphaned child or an injured animal—ready to die in its defense. Onward and upward!

YOURS OF THE 16TH INST. RECEIVED AND CONTENTS NOTED

Your next move is to reply to the publisher's offer. That sounds very simple, but to some writers—particularly to first-time sellers—it is as difficult as finding just the right words to say to a recently bereaved widow.

Enough, already! You're a writer, aren't you? As of today, a professional writer. So write. Say that you are pleased. Thank the editor nicely. Say that you look forward to hearing the terms of the offer. And that's enough, unless the editor has asked some specific questions, in which case you will, of course, answer them. Estimate the length of the finished manuscript, if you are asked to do so. Estimate the date on which you will be able to send in the finished manuscript, if asked—and be both reasonable and specific: Both too short and too long a time are open to suspicion. You may also have been sent some writers' guidelines, detailing the house rules for preparing and submitting manuscripts. Read and understand them, and abide by the ones that apply to you and your book.

In another letter, or by telephone, you will be made an

offer. What kind of offer depends on the kind of publishing house with which you are dealing—a medium-to-large national publisher, a small local press, a specialty house, a package house, whatever. Of one thing you may be certain: Whatever the size or kind of the publishing house, you will not be bowled over by the generosity of the offer. If you are thinking in thousands, think low; if you are thinking in millions, forget it. The cold fact is that this publishing house, or any publishing house, will buy you as cheaply as possible. That, from their point of view, is only good, sound business practice. (When I am working as an editor, I understand this perfectly; when I am working as an author, I still understand it, but it makes me pretty mad.)

Writers tend to think of publishers as fat-cat corporate entities, sitting in their handsome New York offices churning out money like crazy, making numerous laughing-all-the-way trips to the bank. With one hand they crush young, new writers; with the other, they dispense largesse to famous authors. Unless your name is Herriot or Buckley, Michener or Mailer, Wambaugh or Francis, Steele or Le Carré, Ludlum or Dailey, or the like, you don't have a chance. If you are an unknown, even if you write the quintessential book of the ages, nobody will pay the slightest attention.

That is wrong, all wrong from start to finish.

In the first place, although publishers do indeed make money (not surprisingly, they go out of business if they don't), they also spend money. The bigger they are, the more books they put out, the more money they spend. If you feel that "they pay me for my book, then they publish it and everybody pays them for it" covers the whole situation, you are a very simplistic thinker. Here are the chief elements in a publisher's budget for a book:

1. *Acquisition of manuscript.* Payments (advance, royalties) to the author.

2. *Composition.* Getting the book set in type.

3. *PPB.* Paper, printing, and binding, all of which are expensive and all of which must be bought and paid for by the publisher.

4. *Design.* If the book is designed in the house, the cost is included in overhead (see below); if a freelancer designs the book, he/she must be paid.

5. *Illustration.* This is a gray area, in which sometimes the author, sometimes the publisher, foots the bill; sometimes there are no illustrations; at the least, however, the paper jacket of the book must be designed and sometimes illustrated, both of which are expenses of the publisher.

6. *Distribution.* A sales force, either the publisher's own or freelance, must sell the book to libraries, bookstores, and other outlets; the books must be shipped, either to a wholesaler or directly to the individual outlets; books not immediately sold must be warehoused.

7. *Overhead.* The salaries of all the publishing house employees must be paid; the "housekeeping" costs (rent, electricity, cleaning the premises) must be paid.

8. *Taxes and insurance.* Publishers must pay these, like the rest of us.

9. *Advertising and promotion.* If you don't push a book, it doesn't sell; if it doesn't sell, nobody makes any money.

10. *Miscellaneous.* Under this familiar heading come repairs and replacement of furnishings and equipment, rentals of equipment, postage, office supplies, and a dozen other niggling little expenses that can add up to a small fortune.

Who supplies the funds for all this? You do—you and your book.

Suppose that your book sells at retail, in the bookstores, for $16.95 a copy. Ah! you think. Very nice—virtually $17 goes into the publisher's pocket every time someone buys a copy. No way. In the first place, the publisher sells the book to the bookstore at a discount; the bookstore is, after all, in business to make money, as aren't we all. Not $16.95, but instead about $10 goes to the publisher. Before the publisher can tuck the sawbuck into his pocket, however, ten little mouths to feed—the ten points listed above—each take a bite out of it. And that's still not the end of it. Most books are sold on a return basis: If the outlet does not sell the book, it may return it and all bets are off. This returns policy is, admittedly, hedged with safeguards—you can't return a book that looks as if a herd of elephants had been browsing in it, for example, nor can you return one published in 1923 and just discovered in the basement—but nevertheless it exists, and is one more in the long list of expenses.

There is still another. Publishers, being staffed with humans, make mistakes. Like the rest of us, they make a lot of little mistakes that don't count for much in the big scheme of things. But every once in a while a publisher will make a doozie, a lalapalooza, the great grandaddy of all mistakes, and then the excrement really hits the air conditioning.

What kind of mistake? Pick a card—they've all been made

at one time or another. Sometimes a book will be bought, printed, bound, and distributed before anyone notices that this happens not to be the author's book at all but one put out by a totally different publishing company back in 1941. Or if not the entire book, large sections will turn out to be identical with the other author's years-ago effort. This, in case you don't know it, is stealing; the delicate term is "plagiarism." Or it may be a nonfiction book that the author did not plagiarize but made up out of whole cloth, totally ignoring the facts or bending them to suit his fancy. Such a proliferation of error should be caught at an early stage by a bird-dogging copy or line editor, by an on-its-toes legal department, by an expert reader who commands a stiff fee because he *is* an expert. But sometimes the wretched manuscript slips by them all, gets printed and distributed. And *then* somebody yells, "Hey—wait a minute!"

A long time ago I was an editor at a package house that produced, among other things, a line of young-reader books for a major publisher. One day we got in over the transom the manuscript for what looked to be a charmingly old-fashioned book that, the author said in her covering letter, was only one in a long series she had in mind, and which she hoped would become as well known as the Nancy Drew or Tom Swift books. I took it home to read on the weekend and was having fun with it—actually, I decided, it was a skillful send-up of the high-moral-tone books for young readers that were popular years ago—when I began having an uncomfortable sense of déjà vu. The more I read, the more I became certain that I had passed this way before. But where? When? I ran over in my mind the books of my childhood and youth, and found no clue. I went back to the manuscript, finished it, and decided reluctantly to return it to the author the following day. Indeed, it *was* charming. It *was* a skillful send-up. But it was also too familiar for comfort. The problem kept me awake half the night, but by morning I had it: Elsie Dinsmore rides again!

The Elsie Dinsmore books—I don't remember the author or the publisher—were the delight of young girls in my grandmother's day. There were a great many of them, all primly bound in dark-red buckram, printed on paper that would cost a bundle today, and illustrated with engravings of little ladies doing wildly exciting things such as passing the crumpets at tea or greeting the vicar with a well-executed curtsey. The books had lived in our attic when I was a child. I read a couple, and found them the then-equivalent of gross. Somewhere along the line, in the midst of many moves, they disappeared, unmourned. And now here was Elsie again, pretending to be a takeoff when she was actually the real thing, with only character names changed to protect the perpetrator of the scam. No wonder the wretched woman said she had a series in mind! There were enough Elsie Dinsmore books to keep her in comfort for the rest of her life, had she not run across an editor with a memory like an elephant's and a mother with magpie habits. It makes you wonder, though, doesn't it, how many such hoaxes manage to squeeze by unnoticed? And worry about the ones that squeeze by to the printed-and-distributed stage before someone waves a red flag, at which point they become yet another expensive mistake the publisher can ill afford.

Closely akin to the mistakes are the unfortunate accidents. Witness: A short time ago, a respected old publishing house was acquired by another house, the latter with a line of Bibles to sell and a reputation for probity to uphold. The new owners looked over the new acquisition's spring list and found there—tut, tut!—three books whose language offended their delicate sensibilities. "You cannot publish these," they said. Instant chaos. Organizations such as the Authors Guild, the Freedom to Read Committee of the Association of American Publishers, the Dramatists Guild, the Authors League, fired off protests. Scathing editorials appeared. All that mattered not a whit to the publisher, who repeated, "You cannot publish these." The authors of two of the books refused, as was their right, to change the offending language, which was, they maintained, suitable to the plot and characters of the books. Fortunately for everybody, those two books were still in the manuscript stage. Two other publishers stepped forward and offered to buy one each, terms were satisfactorily arranged, and all was well. The third book, however, was already printed and bound. The author sued, which is where the matter stands as this is being written.

Litigation is a fact of life in publishing. Win or lose, litigation costs money—another of the publisher's expenses authors must ultimately pay for.

If all this sounds to you as if, in the constant tug-of-war between authors and publishers, I throw my not inconsiderable weight on the side of the publishers, you are wrong. I have been too long an author, too long entrapped by publishers' wily smiles, too often a victim of their little schemes for that. But I have also been too long an editor, too long chivvied by authors, too much saddened by their sometimes abysmal stupidity, too often taken in by their barefaced untruths, to be entirely on their side, either. I would like to think of myself in any given situation as being on the side of right, no matter how holier-than-thou that may sound. After all, facts is facts, lady, and nobody has to tell the devil to take the hindmost, because he will do so without any prompting from us.

A SPLENDID MOMENT—THE CONTRACT ARRIVES!

Although it may be a long time a-comin', your contract will eventually arrive. There will be three or four copies of it, in blank—that is, unsigned—but with prepared spaces for you to sign as author and someone in authority to sign as representative of the publishing house. Some few publishers still operate on a kind of contract called a "letter of intent," which takes the form of a letter addressed to you and stating briefly that the publishing house intends to publish a book (title or description) of which you are the author, that the manuscript is due (date), and that you will be paid (amount). The letter is signed by an officer of the company, and a space is left for you to sign. Although this is a legal document, it says very little and allows almost uncountable areas for argument, much in the manner of an oral contract sealed by a handshake.

Most publishing contracts, however, are very long documents going on over four, five, six, even seven legal-size pages, spelling out every jot and tittle of the agreement, accounting for every possible contingency, and specifying a remedy for each and every problem that might arise. If this is the first such contract you have ever seen, you may find yourself overcome with a desire to retreat to your bed and pull the covers up over your head. And the fact that you have been sent three, sometimes four, copies of this lengthy document does nothing to allay your apprehension.

But be of good cheer. This contract has been drawn to protect the publisher, but also to protect you. Well, sort of. At the very least, it has been drawn to detail for you exactly what to expect every step of the way, so that you can't say,

"Oh, I didn't know *that!*" or "That was not my understanding."

What do you do with the contract? You sign it—all three or four copies—and return it. In due time you will get back one or two executed—that is, signed by an officer of the company—copies to keep on file. But first, before you even think of signing and returning the contract, you will read it. Slowly. Carefully. Every word of it. When you come to a clause that you don't understand—and there will, believe me, be such clauses—stop and read again; figure it out, and don't go on until you do understand it.

Unless you are very familiar with publishing contracts, you will be wise to have a lawyer read this one before you sign and return it. A word of caution: If at all possible, locate a lawyer familiar with publishing. Lawyers whose area of expertise is taxes or corporate law or forensics or some such are likely to faint dead away on reading their first publishing contract. The reason is simple: Publishing contracts tend to be, not surprisingly, weighted rather heavily in favor of the publisher. Your lawyer, when he picks himself up off the floor, is likely to tell you that the contract is totally unacceptable, and ring for his secretary so he can dictate a letter to the publisher saying so. Restrain him, and ask him to consult a colleague who understands the ins and outs of publishing.

Unless the contract hides some nasty surprises that you missed, some bear traps that can, at some point, clutch you in their wicked jaws, a publishing lawyer will probably say (grudgingly) that the contract is okay, in spite of the fact that it is degrading, demeaning, scandalously cheap, and altogether a disgrace. This may mean that the contract, although legal and without traps, is all of those derogatory things, or it may simply mean that your payment, as stated, does not include the publisher's eyeteeth and a mortgage on his wife and children. What am I saying? This: Get a lawyer's opinion on legality and hidden problems, but reserve to yourself decisions on payments and deadlines. This is your first book; you have very little in the way of ammunition with which to fight. The chief business of an author, the first time around, is to get published. If your first book is successful, you then have a lever with which to pry at the publisher's eyeteeth; a string of successes may even earn you that mortgage. That is not meant to imply that you should sell yourself, first time or not, for a mess of pottage. But be temperate, be reasonable, be sensible. And be published.

WHAT THE CONTRACT IS TRYING TO TELL YOU

Every time I read a publishing contract, I am reminded of the southern belle who loved to tap her suitors with her fan, bat her eyelashes, and exclaim, "Lah, my deah, how you *do* go *on!*" Contracts do go on, offering one bit of obfuscated information after another and then repeating themselves to make certain that they have fouled up the subject sufficiently. Nevertheless, publishing contracts have a great deal to say to you, and you will be well advised to listen carefully.

Although they may in other ways differ from one another considerably, including the order in which clauses are set forth, all publishing contracts worth the paper they're printed on contain the following:

Identification

States that this is an agreement made [date] between [name and address], "hereinafter called the author," and [name and address], "hereinafter called the publisher," to produce a book [brief description to identify the particular book], "hereinafter called the work."

Further Description of "the Work"

For a cookbook, this means the approximate number of recipes, subject(s) to be covered, peripheral material to be supplied by the author, and approximate length of the manuscript, which may be stated as number of words or number of typewritten pages.

Deadline(s)

The date on which the finished manuscript is due in the publisher's office. If the manuscript is to be submitted in halves, both dates will be given; if in quarters, all four dates. These are true due dates, not products of some editor's fancy; they are set up so that, all things being equal (they seldom are), the book will be ready at the time the publisher has advertised it in his catalog.

Restrictions and Options

Most contracts carry a clause forbidding the author to produce a book on the same subject for another publisher within a specified time, which may range from one to five years. Read this carefully. Generally, if you have written a seafood cookbook, for example, you will be restricted from writing a seafood cookbook for another publisher for the next two years. However, it's possible you may discover that if you sign this contract you have agreed not to write *any* cookbook for another publisher for up to five years—obviously a disaster, if you propose to earn your living writing cookbooks, and unfair even if you don't. As for the option clause, it directs you to submit your next book to the publisher who is producing this one, giving him "first refusal." In most cases this is no problem, but there are instances in which it can be. For example, you may have discussed another book with a different publisher, a book on which you have a tentative agreement but as yet no contract. Meanwhile, your finished book—which has been making publishing-house rounds for quite a while—is finally sold, and you have contract in hand, said contract containing a next-book option clause. You should tell the publisher who has bought your present book the conditions surrounding the other one, to avoid later mix-ups. Or perhaps in desperation you sold the present book to the present publisher for terms you feel to be far too low, and would prefer to offer the next book to someone else. The option clause prevents you from doing so. However, if your next book falls in a category far removed from the present one, particularly a category the present publisher never—or seldom—brings out, you can feel fairly certain that the book will be rejected and you'll be free to look for greener pastures. Whatever the circumstances, don't skip lightly over the option clause with a hasty "That'll never happen to me."

Copyright

This is a subject that once gave rise to innumerable bitter altercations when a contract arrived and the author discovered that it provided for the copyright to be taken out in the publisher's name. However, since the enactment of the 1978 copyright law, which (simplified) holds that you, the author, establish your copyright by creation of the manuscript, things have quieted down. Just in case you have fallen into the hands of a publishing sleaze, check the copyright clause to make certain it states that the copyright is yours.

Payments and Periodicity of Payments

Before contract time, you will—I hope—have agreed with the publisher concerning how much and in what manner you will be paid for this book. Now here it is, spelled out in the contract, taking one of several forms:

FLAT FEE. This is a single amount, usually paid in several increments. Flat-fee payments are usually stipulated for a commercial cookbook (for a food producer or a maker of appliances, for example) because such books are not sold in the manner usual with books but are offered as premiums. If you participate in a cookbook anthology, each portion of which is contributed by a different author, you will probably be paid a flat fee for your part in it. On occasion, you may be offered a flat fee by a legitimate (if somewhat slippery) trade book publisher, but this seldom happens.

WRITER FOR HIRE. Sometimes a publisher has an idea for a cookbook and/or a batch of recipes he has come by; the publisher or his employees will outline and flesh out the idea, then a writer familiar with cookbooks will be hired to do the dog-work, and will be paid a flat fee. A second writer-for-hire occasion may arise when a publisher has contracted for a cookbook (generally, in this case, with a well-known writer whose books can be expected to sell well); when the manuscript is submitted, it is a disaster, beyond rescue by general editing. The publisher will then hire another cookbook writer, for a flat fee, to—as it is delicately put—"clean up" the manuscript. I once cleaned up the manuscript of a very well-known, but rapidly aging, author who had omitted something from every single recipe, usually the key ingredient. From her walnut bread she omitted walnuts, from her cranberry chutney she omitted cranberries, from her buttery minted carrots she omitted the butter, and (her best effort) from her sirloin stir-fry she omitted the beef. A useful suggestion: If you are hired to do such a clean-up job, negotiate for a partial by-line. If the book carries "by Josephine Famouslady and Pamela Unknownwriter," you will not only have earned a nice fee, but received an upward boost on the cookbook-writers' ladder.

ROYALTY ARRANGEMENT. This is the most common, and the best, payment deal from the author's point of view and the publisher's as well. The most common version of this system is advance-plus-royalty, under which the author is paid an amount of money in several portions (one third on signing of contract, one third on submission of half the manuscript, one third on completion of manuscript, for example), followed by a percentage of the price of every book sold. Before the royalty checks begin rolling in, the advance must be "earned out"—that is, the amount of the advance must be repaid to the publisher from the author's earnings on the sale of books before those earnings begin to accrue to the author. Royalty percentages are scaled upward, governed by the number of books sold, because by the time the book has sold a specified number of copies the publisher will have earned back his expenses, the author will have earned out the advance, and from there it's gravy all around. On a hardcover book, the common percentage range is 10 percent on the first specified number of books, 12½ percent on the second specified number, and 15 percent thereafter. That "specified number" varies widely, and may go up in increments of 1,000 (on, say, a novel by a first-time writer), 5,000 (on a book with firm but not sky-high expectations), 10,000 (on, perhaps, an expensive-to-produce coffee-table book).

The advance is, in theory, to cover the author's expenses while he writes the book, and it, too, varies considerably, all the way from no advance at all to a very handsome one for the author who is well known, whose book is certain to be successful, even if by reason of his name rather than its own merits. (This, of course, is the author least in need of a subsidy while he writes the book, but whoever said that life is fair?) Your advance on a first cookbook, or first several, may be anything from $2,000 to $7,000. (Julia Child's, I'm told, was $250 on her first book—but that was a long time ago.) If you are aggressive, you may be able to get more than the initial offer. If you have an agent, you will almost certainly get a larger advance than if you do not. If you must live on the advance money while you write the book, obviously you'll want to get as much as the traffic will bear. On the other hand, if you have another income and need only to pay out-of-pocket expenses from the advance, the smaller the advance, the sooner you will be collecting royalties. How well the advance serves you, then, depends on your financial needs versus your faith in the salability of the book. A word here on cookbook advances. Try to get your fee split into two parts: a portion as payment for your work, and a portion to cover expenses, such as food supplies used in testing recipes. Why? Because this split fee will make considerable difference in your taxes.

Paperback originals pay in the same manner—flat fee, writer-for-hire, or advance plus royalties—and for the same reasons. The royalties will be in different percentages, however: Five percent, 6½, and 8 is a middle-of-the-road example. This is because paperbacks are cheaper to produce than hardcover books; being cheaper, they can carry a lower retail price, and carrying a lower retail price, they are likely to sell in much larger quantity than hardcover books. All this being true, the thinking goes, you will get more royalties on a paperback book and so the royalty percentage need not be as high. If you point out that more is not necessarily better if what is referred to is quantity, not quality, that 5 percent on 10,000 is no more than 10 percent on 5,000, prepare to be looked at as if you were a trifle addled. The publishing business is rife with people who carry calculators in their pockets, but apparently they haven't yet learned to use them.

Rights

The book is yours. When a publisher "buys" a book, he is not actually buying it in the sense that it is now his forever and you have relinquished all rights to it. Rather, you are leasing to him certain rights in the book—chief of which is to publish it—and agreeing to share with him certain other rights. Just as you can be penalized if you do not get the manuscript in by the specified deadline, the publisher can be penalized if he does not publish the book in the manner and within the time (commonly two years) specified in the contract.

As for the rights beyond that right to publish, the way in which they are shared must also be carefully spelled out. These—generally called "subsidiary rights"—include first and second serial rights, book club, paperback, film strip, microfilm, computer, stage, record, radio, television, motion picture, and audiovisual rights. Provision must also be made for translation into languages other than English, special editions (premiums, etc.), books sold at less than wholesale (remaindered), and, indeed, such a wriggling can of worms as it is difficult for the uninitiated to imagine.

Of course, all of these rights do not apply to all books. It is unlikely that anyone will wish to make a motion picture or a TV miniseries based on your cookbook (or anyone else's). Translation of a cookbook is such a hoo-hah that it seldom happens: Not only must the words be grouped into felicitous phrases in another tongue, but the recipes must also be revised, because other countries do not use the same battery of measurements that we do and ingredients are often called by totally unlike names. Nor is your cookbook on record or tape likely to make it on the pop charts. Nevertheless, a division of the proceeds from the sale or license of such rights will probably be detailed in your contract, along with a division of the proceeds from rights that could be very important to you indeed.

FIRST SERIAL. Often further defined as "first North American serial," this covers the right to publish (generally in a magazine or newspaper) portions of the book before the entire book is put on sale by the publisher. There can be multiple sales here—that is, first-serial rights to different portions of the book can be sold to different magazines or papers, or a magazine may wish to publish several portions serially or hold them in reserve as editorial fillers. If you have an agent, he may opt to sell first-serial rights, in which case his payment should be the usual one—10 percent of the amount. If you do not have an agent, the publisher may elect (if he's on his toes) to sell these rights, in which case his portion of the proceeds should not be larger than an agent's, but often is.

SECOND SERIAL. Portions of the book, as above, but published *after* pub date—that is, after the entire book is put on sale.

BOOK CLUBS. There are several arts/crafts/cooking book clubs to which rights to publish your book might be sold, and a large number of general book clubs that, under certain conditions—usually concerned with the beauty, unusual quality, and intrinsic worth of the book, as well as the author's name—will offer cookbooks to their readers. Usually it is the publisher who peddles these rights. Often, the decision to offer a book is made by the book club before the book is printed, in which case the number of copies required by the book club can be added to the original print run, thereby cutting the publisher's per-copy cost. Division of the proceeds of a book club license should be 50 percent for the author, 50 percent for the publisher. If you are offered more, smile happily; if you are offered less, yell like a banshee.

PAPERBACK RIGHTS. If your publisher also puts out paperback books, the house may decide to put out a paperback edition of your cookbook. In this case, you will be offered royalties in the same manner as for the hardcover rights, perhaps 5 percent for the first 10,000 copies, 6 percent for the next 10,000, and 7 percent thereafter. The Authors Guild recommends a royalty of two thirds the hardcover rate on a paperback put out by the hardcover publisher—possible, but unlikely.

On a paperback edition of your book published by someone other than the primary publisher—that is, by a paperback house—the proceeds of the license are generally divided neatly in half: 50 percent for the author, 50 percent for the primary publisher; this division usually obtains no matter how many paperback copies are sold. The Authors Guild recommends 50–50 for the first $10,000 of income, 60–40 for the next 10,000, and 70–30 thereafter. Again, unlikely.

Other Clauses

There are other contract clauses worth—as is every aspect of any contract—close examination. These range over as wide a variety of subjects as proceeds from foreign licenses, publisher's bankruptcy, suits for infringement, settling disputes between author and publisher, author's copies, and a host of others. Two, however, require the most meticulous scrutiny on the part of the author before the contract is signed and returned: what is known as the "acceptance clause" and the manner and schedule of payments to the author, including advances but particularly royalties.

"A MANUSCRIPT ACCEPTABLE TO THE PUBLISHER IN FORM AND CONTENT"

The clause that details your deadline(s) will also state that at that time you will deliver a manuscript satisfactory to the publisher, or the same meaning in similar terms. Fine. The publisher has approved your proposal material; the manuscript will be written in the same vein, put together in the same manner—so what could be unsatisfactory about it?

Plenty, as a great many authors have discovered to their sorrow. In the first place, "acceptable" and "satisfactory" are difficult to define when used in this context. These are subjective judgments, similar to our old friend beauty in the eye of the beholder. If it were possible for a manuscript to run a fever, break out in spots, and be pronounced by a competent physician to be a victim of chicken pox, no one would quibble over its unacceptability. But the syndrome of unacceptability in manuscripts is amorphous, exceedingly difficult to pin down; it cannot be heard or seen or smelled or felt—but, to some editors, it is nevertheless there.

Aside from that indefinable quality of "It's good, but I don't like it!" there can be other, more understandable, reasons why a manuscript is deemed to be unsatisfactory. The first is a disaster that can occur to a manuscript of any kind: The editor who fought tooth and nail for the book has moved to another publishing house, and none of the remaining staff were all that crazy about it from the first. Other reasons, although some of them are not applicable to cookbooks, are worth knowing about. Books concerned with politics can easily find themselves in trouble; for example, a book fulsomely praising Richard Nixon's honesty and integrity might have been acceptable before Watergate but certainly not afterward. The reason that publishers of romance novels prefer to see a full manuscript instead of an outline and samples before issuing a contract is that on many occasions, although sample chapters were right on the mark, the remaining chapters turn out to be straight—unacceptable—pornography.

Years ago, just before World War II, while researching something else entirely, I came upon a lot of derogatory material about Lafayette. It was interesting, because almost everything published about Lafayette praises him roundly. I did some more research and then wrote, and sold to *American Mercury,* an article based on the material. I was very pleased with myself: I was young, a beginning writer, and although I had made some sales, I had never sold anything to an outlet half so prestigious as this one. Imagine my joy when, a couple of weeks later, I received a letter from McBride, an equally prestigious publishing house of the time, saying that they had seen the article and were anxious to talk to me about the possibility of a book on the same subject. In due course I called at the McBride office. It was not a good day. Hitler had marched into Austria, and everyone was sick at heart. On my way downtown I had run into one of the great baritones from the Metropolitan Opera, standing on a street corner, tears running down his face, singing "Vienna, City of My Dreams" as I have never heard it sung before or since. I told the editor about it.

"Paris soon." He sighed. "Do you remember what General Pershing said when he reached France during the First World War?"

"Yes. 'Lafayette, we are here!' So—this is not the time to write a book demeaning Lafayette."

"I'm glad you could say that, so I didn't have to."

I thanked him for seeing me, he thanked me for coming, and we parted.

Why did I tell you this story? Well, imagine that, on the day I called on McBride, I had submitted the manuscript of that book instead of simply coming to discuss it. That would have been a totally unacceptable manuscript—not because of authorial negligence nor because of editorial whim, but solely because of calamitous circumstance. That kind of thing—acts of God, acts of war, natural calamities—can be a legitimate reason for deciding that a manuscript is unacceptable. But "This doesn't seem such a hot idea as it once did" or "I never understood why Mary wanted to buy this book" or "I wish Joe had taken this author with him when he went to Doubleday" are not legitimate reasons.

If, in the eyes of the editor, the book walks a fine line between satisfactory and unsatisfactory, can the publisher ask you to revise it? Yes, indeed. But he should give you explicit guidelines, not simply dump it back at you with that time-worn editorial admonition, "This needs a lot of work."

Suppose, after you have made revisions to the best of your ability, the publisher still declares the manuscript to be unsatisfactory and demands, as per the contract, that you return a portion (or the whole) of the advance paid you. What can you do? Well, you can sue—an expensive nuisance, win or lose. And you are not likely to win, because "satisfactory" and "acceptable" are matters of subjective judgment. You (or, preferably, your lawyer) can negotiate with the publisher; if you can show that, in spite of the editor's "unsatisfactory" verdict, you followed all of his or her instructions in preparation of the manuscript and that the manuscript is indeed of the same kind and quality as the proposal material the editor accepted, and that you revised in good faith as per his or her guidance, you may still have the manuscript rejected but you may be allowed to keep the portion of the advance already paid you, despite the fact that your contract says you must return the advance in full if the manuscript is rejected.

In deeming a manuscript "unacceptable" because it is "unsatisfactory," the criteria the publisher uses are supposed to be totally editorial. In other words, the publisher is saying, in effect, that the manuscript, in style and content, is not professionally competent and is therefore unfit for publication. Other considerations are not supposed to color this decision —for example, that the manuscript, which looked so eminently salable when the contract was made, now appears unsalable because of circumstances outside the author's and the publisher's control. This might happen with a political book if in the intervening time a new law were passed that would temper the thrust of the book's premise or, with a medical book, if a discovery were made that would make obsolete most of the book's information.

Such things are not supposed to affect the book's acceptability. In theory, at least, only if you, the author, have made a real mess of things can the book be rejected as unsatisfactory, unacceptable.

"THE CHECK IS IN THE MAIL"

Another area in which author and publisher may come to—at least verbal—blows concerns royalty statements and the attendant checks for royalties. The seat of the quarrel is generally not that the statements are wrong (although they can be, including errors in simple arithmetic), but that they do not appear when expected, sometimes do not appear long after they are expected, and sometimes do not appear at all.

Quarterly statements, covering three months of the year, can be expected to arrive during the following quarter—preferably about the middle of the quarter but more realistically near the end of it. Thus, the statement for the term January through March will appear during the following May or June. Why not April? Because some of the business of the previous quarter will not be finished—sales figures will not be complete, returns figures will not be accurate. If you get a statement early in March for the quarter just past, you can safely bet that it will be pretty far removed from the actual figures and may deliver you a nasty blow when revised in the following statement.

So, May rolls by, and no statement. Don't panic. June arrives, bringing roses and gentle breezes, but no statement. The weather heats up and so, as the end of June approaches, do you. Drop the publisher a brisk note, pointing out that your January–March statement has not yet arrived; it won't do you a lot of good, but may ease your blood pressure somewhat. Early the next month, after the Fourth of July festivities are over, the statement will probably appear. If it doesn't, make loud noises. If it still doesn't, have your lawyer send one of his inimitable see-here-now letters. By your contract, if it's worth the paper it's written on, you can—as a last resort—send an independent auditor to go over the publisher's books. Publishers hate this, not because they have fudged the books but because it makes for extra work and assorted hassles; independent auditors tend toward arrogance, and when they have right on their side the arrogance knows no bounds. Of course, if the publisher *has* fudged the books, his screams of innocence will be heard by the aborigines in the far reaches of the Australian outback. But this practically never happens. Spiritually, like all the rest of us, publishers know that honesty is the best policy. Practically, the amounts of money involved simply aren't worth all that trouble.

If by chance you have signed a contract that gives you a royalty on the first printing, a somewhat higher one on the second printing, and a still higher one on subsequent printings (I beg you, from the bottom of my heart, not to sign such a contract, *ever*!), getting an understandable statement from the publisher will fall in roughly the same class as your chances of finding the Hope diamond while you're taking the dog for his morning stroll. To begin with, print orders—the number of copies of a book printed—are the publisher's, all publishers', secret. They will auction off their wives and children rather than part with that holy figure, do battle, bleed and die to protect it, relinquish their sacred honor before revealing it.

I have attended many a pub meeting in which the following ridiculous scene has taken place.

PUBLISHER: Well, we had better—uh—set the—uh—p.o. *(As if everyone in the room didn't know what those initials stand for.)*

SALES MANAGER: Ummmmmm.

PUBLISHER: Well, let's see. *(He tears a piece of paper from a scratch pad, scribbles on it, folds it twice, and passes it to the sales manager.)*

SALES MANAGER: Ummmmm. *(He unfolds the paper, stares at it, turns white as a sheet, begins to tremble.)* No, Joe. No, no! *(He scratches out the figures on the paper, substitutes others, and passes the paper back.)*

PUBLISHER *(staring at paper)*: Oh. Ah. Um. *(He tears the paper into tiny bits, flutters them into his wastebasket, takes a fresh paper, writes on it, and passes it over to the sales manager.)*

SALES MANAGER *(unfolding the paper)*: Ummmmm. Too rich for my blood, Joe. Too rich for my blood. *(He revises the figures, returns the paper.)*

(This goes on for several more exchanges. At long last they come to a meeting of minds, if that is the word I'm looking for.)

PUBLISHER: Well, fine. That's settled. Now, what's next on the agenda?

I repeat: Do not sign a contract based on unspecified print orders. That way lies madness.

One more cautionary note concerning royalty statements. There may be—probably will be—an item called "publisher's reserve." Or the reserve may be built into the statement elsewhere, but it will exist in one form or another. I am not saying that the publisher's reserve should not exist, but only warning you that it does so you will not be taken aback by it, and so when you crab about it (this is a favorite topic when authors get together) you'll know what you're crabbing about. The reserve is a portion of royalties held back by the publisher to cover returns that may not yet be in at the time the statement is issued.

Why do authors complain? Because the amount of the reserve, in many cases, seems horrendously high, appears to be more than enough to cover all copies of the book out. And because—the reason most authors complain about royalty statements in general—it appears that the publisher has the use of (and, presumably, collects the interest on) the author's money long after it ought to be earning interest for the author.

YOU'RE NOT THROUGH YET

Once the main business of writing a book has been accomplished, you may feel that you can rest your oars and drift. Although your complete manuscript has been sent to the publisher by deadline, and although in due course (a long course, as usual) the manuscript has been accepted, quite a few small tidy-ups remain before you can truthfully say you are through.

First, as the publisher's editor goes through the book, armed with a blue pencil in one hand and a fine-tooth comb in the other, he or she will probably come across a number of places where he or she feels revisions are called for, and will ask you to make such revisions. Make them, with good grace, unless they change something already right to wrong (editors who know nothing about cooking will sometimes ask for such changes) or will cause a serious departure from the theme and thrust of the book. If you do not wish to make the changes, write to the editor saying so and explaining fully. Some requested changes, you may feel, will make the revised section different, but in no way improve it. This sort of thing is what is known as editorial prerogative (a distant relative of poetic license). Go ahead—be a sport and make the changes. It is editors' business to edit, and some don't feel that they are earning their salaries (known as "making my contribution to the book") unless they do. Not all editors by any means have this attitude. Many edit what needs editing, and keep their hands off what doesn't.

Suppose that you are asked to make major revisions that may change the entire concept of the book and amount to virtually a complete rewrite. Now what? You have several choices, none of them particularly palatable. First, you can—if you can afford to, both financially and in terms of your reputation—say no, return the advance you have already received, and try to peddle the book elsewhere. This is not a choice I advocate, but if it is yours, at least don't do it in the heat of anger. Give yourself a week to cool off and to think it through.

It is entirely possible, of course, that you may agree with the editor that what he suggests will improve the book greatly. If so, roll up your sleeves and go to work. Follow the editor's suggestions faithfully, and if you get stuck, call for guidance; after all, this is his idea, so he ought to know what to do next.

Between the extremes of these two choices lie two others. If you are very anxious to prevent this manuscript from being rejected as unsatisfactory, even if you don't agree with the editor's suggestions you can swallow your pride and the gall that rises in your throat, and go ahead to make the revisions as requested. Or you can put up a fight—just make sure, before you fire your first salvo, that you have your campaign well thought out. Write to the editor, carefully detailing your objections to the revision requests, point by point. Shoot him down whenever and however you can. But don't, *don't*, lose your temper, or at least don't let it show. If you do the job well, you may—surprisingly—win, although I admit that your chances of winning are in direct relation to the number of successful books you've previously had published. But even without a published book to your name, if right is on your side you still may win. The editor may only have been flexing his editorial muscles, and truthfully not give a damn. Or he may not have any greater faith in his ideas than you have, and know that if you withdraw the book he will have to explain why to his superiors, in the course of which explanation the whole controversy will come out and be judged, not necessarily in his favor.

However, win or lose, don't fall into the trap of believing that your book, just because it is yours, is writ in blood, engraved in stone. You may, indeed, be an excellent writer. But out there somewhere are better writers. One of the huge fallacies of the publishing business goes, So-and-so wrote it, therefore it must be good. Nonsense! Bad writers write bad books, but good writers also write bad books, the difference being that the good writers' bad books get on bestseller lists, sometimes as many as three or four in a row before anyone notices. The writer who falls so madly in love with his own deathless prose that he can't bear to allow one comma to be changed is at a serious disadvantage. Editors hate him, and he brings a lot of unnecessary suffering on himself because the manuscript that goes through without one comma changed has yet to be written.

Which brings us to the next person who has a whack at your manuscript, the copy editor, whose job it is to tidy up spelling and grammar and syntax. Some writers—good ones, established ones—who take the editor's workings with good grace go absolutely crazy when the copy editor gets loose. Generally, the copy-edited manuscript is returned to the author so that queries can be answered, comments made, and rebuttal engaged in. Every copy editor has his/her own particular dislikes: some cannot abide split infinitives, others are made ill by dangling participles, others abhor the passive voice, still others foam at the mouth over sentences ending in a preposition.

Because writers are more interested in getting their thoughts down on paper than in the fine points of structure, the copy editor can be anything from a necessary evil to a writer's salvation. But an overzealous copy editor can take all the grace and guts out of a manuscript, leaving it correct but sterile.

Publishing cherishes a lot of copy-editor stories. I once copy-edited a children's book in which I automatically changed "Why did you bring that book up?" to "Why did you bring up that book?" Back came the manuscript from the author with the sentence changed again. Now it read: "What did you bring the book I didn't want to be read to out of up for?" A copy editor who corrected a split infinitive in one of James Thurber's manuscripts found scribbled in the margin of the returned manuscript, "When I split an infinitive it's damned well going to stay split!" To an overfinicky copy editor, Winston Churchill sent this marginal note: "This is the sort of nonsense up with which I will not put."

In spite of the horror stories, copy editors, although some suffer from overrefinement, generally do a good job. When your copy-edited manuscript is sent to you, carefully answer all the queries, read through the corrections, and unless they are either silly or wrong, leave them.

After you have returned the manuscript to the publisher, there will be a time lapse while the manuscript is set in type. When that is done, you will be sent proof to read, either in the form of long, unwieldy strips of paper called "galley proof" if the publisher is still having books set in hot metal, or as photocopies of page-size type if the publisher has books set by computer.

Your job now is to read the proof carefully and correct any errors you find. Errors in proof are of two kinds—those made by the printer in the course of setting the type and those made by the author and editors in the course of writing and subsequent tinkering with the manuscript. The correction of each error is charged for: Those made by the printer (known as "printer's errors," or PEs) are corrected by him without charge to the publisher, but all other changes (known as "author's alterations," or AAs, and "editor's alterations," or EAs) must be paid for. The publisher absorbs the charges for errors made by his staff (EAs) and will also pay for a portion of the proof changes made by the author—generally, the percentage the publisher will hold still for is spelled out in your contract. Beyond that limit, if you wish further changes you must pay for them, and the charge will be deducted from royalties due you.

Technically, in that wonderful world of perfection for which we are all striving so mightily, there should be no errors, other than PEs, in the proof. Don't hold your breath. There will be some outright mistakes, and these must be corrected. There will be some sentences that appall you, some passages you won't be able to believe that you wrote. You will decide you were never meant to be a writer, that you ought to take up plumbing or bricklaying or some other job more suited to your talents. This is a set of symptoms that attacks all writers, and attacks the writer of a first book in a particularly virulent form. It will pass. Not too long from now you will be saying, as writers have who came before you and writers will who come after you, "My, it certainly reads better when it gets into print, doesn't it?"

A word about copy-editing, a skill it wouldn't hurt every writer to acquire. (Beats hell out of waiting tables during dry spells.) Copy editors are a breed apart. The majority of them are middle-aged or elderly ladies—and when I say "ladies" I mean it. They are well educated, well read, skilled particularly in all the arts of English. They are by bent of mind picky, picky, picky, and their job requires them to learn to be pickier still. They read copy vigilantly, pounce on errors with unconcealed glee. They don't all wear arch-preserver shoes and neat little lace collars, but they appear to be doing so. Do I scorn them? No, I envy them. They love their work and they do it well, two excellent attributes. I was never able to hold a copy-editing job for long, because although I have the skills, my nature is to set fire to a bad manuscript rather than tidy it up.

One of those skills is the ability to understand and use a set of special marks to guide the printer in his typesetting. Even if you never copy-edit for fun and profit, a knowledge of these marks can serve you or any writer well, if only because it helps you to understand the copy-edited manuscripts sent to you for approval. A chart of these marks appears on page 201.

CLOSING IN ON PUB DATE

While you are waiting for your book to burst full blown on an unsuspecting world, get on with your life. Start work on your second book. Or write a couple of articles (remembering that you can now add to your credentials, "My seafood cookbook, *Minnows to Whales,* will be published by Snodgrass, Jukes, and McGillacuddy this coming October"). Or, if your financial back is to the wall, get a job; if not, do some volunteer work. Whatever. But don't just sit there. Waiting for something to happen is one of mankind's most futile pastimes, because it slows the passing of time rather than hastening it. Fill the hours, preferably with something profitable or at least useful, and before you know it your book will be on sale and you can truthfully answer, "I'm an author!" when someone asks what you do.

Chapter Seven

Mixed Bag: Advertising, Promotion, Perks, Freebies, and Other Matters

There are many small events, both expected and unexpected, concomitant to the publishing of most books, and cookbooks are no exception. Some are thoughtfully planned, others occur willy-nilly. Some require a burst of effort on your part, others nothing but your passive presence. Some few may reduce you to tears, but most will cause fits of laughter. Some may be embarrassing, but most will be matters for pride and self-congratulation.

Of course, not all of these will be your lot with a first book. Some may never come your way. There are crowds of writers who escape participation in any such goings-on, just as there are professional golfers who never in their long careers have hit a hole in one, police officers who never in all their years of service have drawn their guns, women who in a lifetime of waiting and hoping never have managed to meet Mr. Right. Those things do happen. But—fortunately or unfortunately—not often.

Some of the events are a lot of fun, some boring. The important thing to remember is that every time you show yourself in public, in whatever manner, you are helping to sell your book. So paste a smile on your face, pour honey into your voice, and carry on. If you're an extrovert—or, as it is fashionable to say today, exhibit type-A behavior—you'll enjoy the whole process. If you are an introvert, force yourself. From the smallest to the largest, these peripheral doings that surround the publishing of a book are important, and when it is required you should give wholehearted cooperation.

THE PUBLISHER GETS THE BALL ROLLING

Some publishers believe that advertising is the way to sell their product, and build hefty advertising allotments into each book's budget. At the other extreme are those who rely on their sales force to sell the book to stores and other outlets, and count on reviews, publicity, and word of mouth to sell to the public, maintaining that advertising is a waste of money and has no effect whatever on the sale of any given book.

Virtually all publishers advertise in *Publishers Weekly* twice a year, touting their spring and fall lists in ads that may run to many pages if the house is a big one with a long list. Your book will doubtless be among those showcased in one of those ads. To some publishers, this is both the beginning and the end of advertising. To others, it is only the beginning: they advertise either single books or several at once in such outlets as *The New York Times Book Review* and other similar weekly newspaper supplements, in *Publishers Weekly* at times other than the big semiannual spring- and fall-list issues, and in magazines such as *West Coast Review of Books*, *The Writer*, and *Writer's Digest.* Scholarly books may be advertised in upscale periodicals, romance fiction in the several magazines devoted to that genre and perhaps in allied publications, such as *Soap Opera Digest.* Top-flight novels are advertised on the book pages of newspapers during the week, and in magazines such as *Harper's* and *Atlantic Monthly.* How-to books appear in everything from *Popular Mechanics* to *Needlecraft.* For all I know, suitable books (*Unarmed Combat for Fun and Profit*?) are advertised in such periodicals as *Soldier of Fortune* and *Mercenery.* Certainly a multitude of outlets exists in which book advertising is suitable.

And cookbooks? They, too, are well suited to advertising in several kinds of publications. One publishing house that specializes in cookbooks does an all-out job. They have contracted for the fourth (back) cover of *Publishers Weekly* three weeks out of each four, and their cookbooks—generally one at a time—are advertised there to the bookstores and other outlets. When the book goes on sale, it is advertised on the food pages of the author's hometown newspaper, in food-oriented magazines such as *Bon Appetit*, *Gourmet, Cuisine,* and *Cook's Magazine,* as well as in women's and shelter magazines such as *Good Housekeeping, Better Homes and Gardens, House Beautiful, McCalls, Ladies' Home Journal,* and the like. At the same time, this publishing house is busily promoting the book in several other ways.

Do they sell books? Indeed they do, in quantities for each book unbelievable to other publishers. Do their authors make money? Indeed they do, although not in the amounts you might imagine. The publishing house adheres to the standard 10–12½–15 percent royalty scale, but the author must pay for the illustrations and those illustrations are taken under strict guidelines of the publishing house. The bill for all those pictures can run as much as $25,000; add to that the (modest) advance, and in spite of all the advertising hoopla it is a fair time before the author begins to collect royalties. The book is kept in print, however, and the publishing house continues to push it, so that as with all good stories this one has a happy ending. Except for this sour note: The management has recently undergone a complete turnover, and no one knows in what direction the new people will move.

PROMOTING AND PUBLICIZING

That which is for free can be, as we all know, the best of bargains. This is as true in the book business as in any other field.

Every large publishing house has one or two or several promotion people whose job it is to get as much free publicity as possible for the books it publishes. This effort is directed largely toward editors of papers and magazines and services people at radio and television networks and stations, but encompasses anyone who can be expected to give a book a good word and a pat on the back. Almost all newspapers have book-review pages, some have special book sections, and some have both—the former during the week, the latter as a Sunday supplement. Many newspapers also have special once-a-week sections devoted to advertising and articles on particular subjects, such as fitness, health and beauty, food, and so on. It is the food section, usually quite hefty, on which promotion people pushing cookbooks zero in. Likewise, many magazines review books; women's magazines, and to a lesser extent shelter magazines, devote a large portion of their pages to food—recipes, new products, new appliances, cooking techniques, and so on—and here a promotion person will try to find a home for information about your cookbook.

To get the attention of these media editors, publicity people turn themselves inside out. For many books, a press kit is prepared, an impressive-looking folder in which will be housed a copy of the book and which may also contain such items as an author bio, a Q&A about how the book came to be written, the history of the recipes if they have a history, perhaps the jacket or cover of the book blown up to poster size if its attractiveness warrants such treatment, a wall chart of a blown-up piece of information from the book, such as a rundown of exotic fruits, a time-and-temp chart for barbecuing, or the like—anything and everything that will get an editor's attention and persuade him or her to use the material in a feature story about the book and the author.

Book tours are another form of promotion. Authors are whisked around the country by the publisher's promotion person, going on a prearranged schedule from talk show to talk show, interview to interview, bookstore to bookstore. On such a tour, you seldom know where you are when you wake up in the morning. Indeed, you're lucky if you can remember *who* you are. For the young, energetic, healthy, and aggressive author, such tours can be fun; for others, they are a foretaste of hell. Cookbook authors, particularly first-timers, are seldom treated—if that's the word—to such tours, unless the book can be, by lucky coincidence, tied to a nationwide food promotion of some kind. Such tours can be very expensive, and it is finally dawning on book houses that they do little other than massage the author's ego. In other words, they don't sell all that many books, and selling books is what publishing is all about.

By-telephone trips are a variation of the author-tour idea.

A series of phone interviews is set up by the publisher's promotion/publicity people. A schedule of these is supplied to the author, and a press kit to the person who will do the interview, generally the host of a radio talk show or cooking show. At the proper moment, as detailed in the schedule, the author puts in a long-distance call to the station, phone number supplied by the schedule, and identifies him- or herself. If you are lucky, the station will have been informed about the imminent phone call; unlucky, you'll have to—quickly—explain the situation. Then you'll be put on the host's phone line, on hold. Presently you will hear him or her say, "This morning we have with us Portia Finkelbank of Kalamazoo, Michigan, whose wonderful new cookbook, *Eggs I Have Known,* has just been published by Persnickety Press. Good morning, Portia."

Go ahead—say "Good morning!" nicely to the gentleman (if that be the case). You're on the air. If heaven is on your side, the host will have at least looked through your book, have some idea of what it's about, and be prepared to ask you a few intelligent questions. If not, you'll have to fend for yourself, without much help other than an occasional "Um" or "Ah" from the host. Either way, your job is to plug the book, to make it sound so fascinating that the listeners can't wait to rush out and buy it. Repeat the title a number of times, to fix it in their minds; ditto the name of the publisher. Talk about a couple of the truly humdinger recipes, so the listeners will want to try them. Exit gracefully, with gracious thank-yous to the host, but not until you get a cue to do so: Shows are timed, and if you leave the host with a couple of minutes of empty air on his hands, he'll be grumpy and spend the spare time closing you out in a tone of voice—sometimes in words—which makes it clear that the moment he got rid of you was his life's happiest.

Such by-phone interviews can have a chilling impersonality to them. You know only the interviewer's name. If you can tell his sex from the name, fine, but in these days of unisex names, this often doesn't work. Sometimes even the voice won't clue you. If he's not very forthcoming, put some of the onus on him by asking, "Do you cook, Mr. Saddlebag?" If he says yes, ask his area of expertise and point out some recipes in your book that he might like to try. If he says no—well, forge ahead, and better luck next time. Be prepared for surprises. If he is familiar with the city from which you are calling, he may ask you the name of your favorite restaurant, or if Joe's Bar is still down there on Fourth Street. If he was at loose ends last night he may have done a bit of boning up, and throw into the conversation such tidbits as, "Can you tell us a little about the poison that occurs in your West Coast mussels this time of year?" or "I understand that lemonade was an Arab invention—is that true?" or "There's a wonderful story about the planting of olives in California—do you know it?" Keep your cool, trying not to sound as if a bomb had just exploded in your face. If you know the answer, go ahead. Briefly. If you don't, you have two courses open to you, both fraught with traps. "No, I don't. Please tell me!" or "Oh, I don't think we have time to go into that, Mr. Saddlebag, it's such a long and complex matter." Either way, *bon chance,* kiddo.

If you are a reasonably verbal person, poised, well versed in your subject, you should have little trouble with these author-tour interviews, whether by phone or in person. But be on your toes. Anything can happen, and certainly will. I once, long ago, spent an hour and a half every morning, five days a week, running a talk show on a radio station. I coped with mornings when the typist had lost my copy, with an engineer who half the time forgot to turn on my microphone, with interviewees who had talked a blue streak before the show but who couldn't be coaxed into opening their mouths once we were on the air. I delivered little homilies on pregnancy (I was eighteen years old and unmarried), on how to hold a man (I didn't have one), on ballet (I hate it), on opera (I love it, but didn't know much about it), on acting and the theater (at last, something I did know about!), on religion (I fancied myself an atheist at that time), on art (I may not know anything about art, but I know what I like), on fashion (firmer ground—I had done some modeling, emceed some fashion shows, and was a devoted follower of *Vogue* and *Harper's*), and dozens of other topics, most of them strangers till we met. With that background, I was reasonably well prepared for tours and by-phone interviews, and can't give you any really helpful advice if you are by nature shy and reclusive, other than "Chin up!" and "This, too, shall pass."

Whatever else you are asked to do to promote your book, you're very likely to be invited to stage a bookstore autograph party. You'll sit in the bookstore, beside a pile of your books, and meet your public. If all goes well, a goodly number of the books will be purchased, during which transactions you'll smile, chitchat, generally demonstrate what a lovely person you are—and sign the books that are sold. These autograph sessions (I prefer that word to "parties") usually last a matter of two or three hours and can be very pleasant—provided, as I said before, all goes well. What can go wrong? Well, the promotion person who set up the autograph session may have neglected to arrange for sufficient publicity calling attention to the event. In that case, no one will come, which can be devastating to the ego of even the most self-confident author. Or the bookstore people may have forgotten that they ordered only three copies of your book and two of those have previously been sold. When crowds of potential buyers turn up—and in these circumstances I can guarantee you that crowds *will* turn up—there will be no books to sell, and embarrassment all around. Because it is difficult to get across to the public that bookstores stock only what they order, and because the publicity person will have vanished at the first whiff of trouble, the whole sorry affair will turn out to be your fault, and you will find yourself apologizing profusely for something entirely out of your control.

Once, when I was trapped in such a circumstance, I remembered that there was another bookstore at the far side of this same shopping mall, one whose manager was a good friend of mine and who could be counted on to have ordered a generous supply of my new book for old times' sake. Trailing a cheerful gang of book buyers behind me, I marched across the mall, explained hastily to my manager friend, and sat down to autograph books. But you can't count on such serendipity more than once in a hundred times. The other ninety-nine there's nothing to do but grin and bear it.

FORTUNATE FALLOUT

Some nice things, very nice indeed, can happen to you as the author of a book, whether it is your first or twenty-first.

Windfall income is one of them. First- or second-serial rights, or both, may be sold. A book club may choose your book as an alternate selection, or even the main selection.

The book may win an award, which is not only pleasant but also generally sells books. A paperback house, or the paperback operation of the publisher who produced your hardcover book, may decide to put out a paperback edition. Or someone—such as a bank, an insurance agency, a kitchen appliance manufacturer, or any one of a dozen other firms—may purchase a premium edition to give away to its customers. If the first printing of your book sells well, it will be sent back to press. All of these possibles result in more money for you.

But money, lest you forget, is not everything. Other nice things will happen, things that bring you recognition and prestige (which, if your mind is stuck in a rut, can even be transmogrified into money down the road a piece—when you write another book, for example, or when you apply for a particular job). You will find, as a small example, that you are all at once exceedingly popular with committees in charge of bake sales, food bazaars, and the like. More importantly, if you make yourself, or allow yourself to be made, just a wee bit conspicuous, you'll find yourself being asked to speak to groups like women's clubs, writers' circles, book-review gatherings, and such. The prestige grows every time you open your mouth, and such speaking engagements sell books, too.

You may also be asked to appear on local radio and television programs, not specifically to promote your book but because you are an interesting person—all persons who write, you'll discover, are interesting persons. You may be asked to talk about a particular facet of food/cooking, or you may—on television—be asked to do some cooking demonstrations. Or, once local TV and radio people learn that you are charming, witty, and intelligent, and that your face doesn't crack the lens of the TV camera, you may be asked to appear on panel and/or talk shows whose subject for discussion is far removed from the kitchen.

Ideas spark new ideas. While your book is still in the public eye, you'll certainly want to write an article, or two or three or four, for one of the food magazines, or a service or shelter magazine that is food oriented, or even a general magazine if you can come up with an idea that intrigues its editors.

If you have a reasonably good voice, know what you're talking about, and are well coordinated, you may be asked to do cooking demonstrations at department stores or fancy appliance stores, or to be one of a series of featured demonstrators at a cooking school. Or you may be asked to teach a particular facet of cooking, such as wok cookery, using a microwave oven, using a food processor or other appliance, making puff pastry or yeast breads—there are classes in anything and everything at night schools, community colleges, and various kinds of vocational schools.

During the spring and summer quarters last year, I taught a course called "Cookbooks: From Kitchen to Bookstore" at the University of California. It led students through the necessary steps in putting together and selling a cookbook. Before the first meeting of the class, I envisioned a collection of girls, with a sprinkling of boys, all looking for a couple of quick/easy credits. But to my gratified surprise I drew a much more interesting mix. There were women—and some men, as well—who had "always wanted to write a cookbook but didn't know how to get started." There were caterers who proposed to write a cookbook and were looking for professional advice. There were chefs and restaurant cooks who had not reached chef status eager to put their expertise on paper—and sell it, of course. There was a food photographer and three food copywriters from advertising agencies, all looking to pick up useful tips. And a large number of people had joined the class because they were about to embark on one or another kind of community fund-raiser cookbook, and didn't know where to begin.

It is doubtless dawning on you by now that publishing a cookbook can lead you in one of many directions, if you will let it. And there are more. If you know your grammar, syntax, and spelling as well as you do your soufflés, sauces, and quick breads, there are openings for good, even-handed cookbook editors. Or you might want to start a cooking school of your own. Or you might decide to branch out and become a caterer or a restaurant cook. It all depends on your skills and your areas of interest. There are some minor drawbacks to all this. People will telephone you at all hours in search of detailed directions for making duck pâté. You can work up a dandy guilt trip if you buy a birthday cake instead of baking it, no matter how tired and busy you are. And even your dearest friends, fearful of being embarrassed, will stop asking you to dinner.

HIGH—AND LOW—SOCIETY

Socially, your status will improve when your book is published. I don't mean merely that you will have more to talk about at the semimonthly meeting of the Bookworm Society. Most of the people you meet in the course of any of the happenings we've been talking about will be interesting, and some of them are likely to become good friends. Because, among most groups of people, like calls to like, you may wish to join one or several of the many local and national writers' organizations. There you will meet congenial people, people with ideas and ambitions and dreams that are like your own. All over the country there are writers' conferences where new friends can be made, ideas exchanged, and contacts cultivated.

Whether you live in a big city or a small town, grapevines will be flourishing, and the fact that you have published a cookbook will spread around in no time. People will stop you to talk on the street, or strike up a conversation on a bus. They will, amazingly, know not only that you've published a book, but also intimate details of your private life. A perfect stranger—well, imperfect actually—will consult you on whether the strawberry season has now reached its peak, and then segue into "I do hope that your sister has reconciled with her husband—broken marriages are so hard on the children!" You'll have to learn how to deal with strangers like that—short of knocking their teeth down their throats.

It is in the supermarket, any supermarket, that you will have your widest—and wildest—variety of contacts with strangers. Most of these people turn out to be pleasant, but invariably there will be a few who don't have both oars in the water, so be on your toes. The majority will simply identify themselves and say that they bought your book and are enjoying it. A few will want to discuss at length the recipe on page 127; be patient and polite—this is your audience. But some will engage you in long conversations. Just the other day, a woman stopped me in the produce section to say, "Excuse me, but I can't help asking—why are you buying one yellow squash, two zucchini, one tomato, and that little eggplant? None of them is enough for more than one person, and I know—"

She was about to tell me that I had a husband, a fact of

which I was already aware. So I interrupted with "I'm going to make ratatouille, and because we're going out of town tomorrow, I don't want a lot of leftovers."

"Oh. Uh—rata-what?"

So I launched into a recipe for ratatouille, while she took notes. The greengrocer sidled up and reminded me in a stage whisper, "Don't forget the onions." Another customer threw in that, although it wasn't traditional, she always put green beans in her ratatouille. Another remarked that although she would like to include them, she left out mushrooms because her kids wouldn't eat them. It turned into quite a kaffee-klatsch.

In New York, my after-work forays into the market often coincided with those of a TV newsman with whom I had a slight acquaintance. Generally we nodded, said "good evening," and passed each other by. But one evening he brought for my inspection a red snapper. I pointed out that the flesh was firm, the eyes unclouded, and that there was no old-fish smell, so the snapper was probably fine. Prompted by further questions, I told him how to make a lemon-butter-parsley stuffing for his catch, and how to cook it. The next few times we met, we simply good-eveninged each other again, but soon he was there with a piece of fresh salmon. I told him to tie it in cheesecloth—"The cheesecloth is over there, in aisle four"—and poach it in a mixture of white wine, water, onion, and celery. "Measure the fish at its thickest point," I told him, "and poach it ten minutes for each inch of depth." Then, caught up in my subject, I gave him instructions for making hollandaise in a blender.

After that we were fast friends, although we never said a word to each other that didn't have to do with food and cooking until one evening, in a burst of excitement, he confided that tonight, after the braised lamb with mushrooms and herb-broiled eggplant, he was going to ask the woman to whom he'd been feeding these delicacies for the past several months to marry him. I didn't encounter him again, because that was the last night for me in New York, before we moved to San Diego. But I know, from the grapevine, that the young man is married. I hope he's happy. And I'd like to convey now what I neglected to tell him then: You're really better off not buying meat and fish at a supermarket, even a very good supermarket. There's an excellent butcher shop two blocks north, on the corner of Fiftieth Street, and an equally good fish market over on Second Avenue at Fifty-second.

BEST OF ALL, IT'S FOR FREE

One of the pleasant bits of fallout from doing a cookbook is the freebies that may come your way. Admittedly, these are more frequent and more lavish when you do a commercial cookbook, but a trade book can have its goodies, as well.

Suppose that you are going to do a cookbook based on a particular kitchen appliance—a blender, say, or a food processor or a slow cooker or a toaster oven or whatever. Your first move should be to determine what's on the market and how each of the available appliances works and how they differ from one another. You can, of course, hang around the appliance department of a well-stocked department or specialty store, but this makes the salespeople nervous after the first hour, and you can only look, not test. Instead, write to manufacturers, saying that you are starting work on a cookbook centered around blenders (you're better off if you can say "a cookbook to be published this coming autumn by Half-diddle Books"), that you wish, of course, to include their blender in the text and would appreciate having one to use in testing recipes. You will shortly be knee deep in blenders or whatever.

Some manufacturers, in the covering letter, after many polite good wishes will give you an address to which the blender should be returned when you are through with it. (Why, I can't imagine—a blender that has lived through a recipe-testing session is secondhand, to say the least. I like to think, charitably, that such manufacturers donate them to convalescent homes, orphanages, and the like.) If no such address is given, when you are through testing call or write the company and ask where the blender should be returned. If you don't, it's possible that so long a time later that you've forgotten all about it, you'll be served with a summons to appear in small claims court to account for one missing blender. Don't laugh—it isn't funny.

It is much more likely, however, that the company will be utterly flummoxed by the very suggestion, tell you to keep it and enjoy it. Shortly, there you will be, surrounded by eighteen slightly used blenders. Does your mother have a good blender? Your mother-in-law? Your sister, your friends, the church kitchen, the senior citizens center? Distribute the largesse and enjoy the feeling of being Lord or Lady Bountiful.

More often than not, food companies err on the side of overgenerosity. On various occasions, I have possessed enough unflavored gelatin to solidify the Pacific Ocean, sufficient tomato sauce to throw a spaghetti dinner for the entire state of California, and a dozen other appalling overabundances, all because assorted food-company executives have said to their secretaries, "Be sure to send Mrs. Townsend some of our product to use in testing." I was once the stunned recipient of five pounds of jasmine tea. Have you any idea of the volume of tea? Five pounds brewed would fill an Olympic-size pool, and jasmine tea is a sometime thing, not a beverage to be enjoyed three times a day.

The most appreciated of such windfalls came shortly after we moved from New York to San Diego. In preparation for the move I had shut my eyes, hardened my heart, and thrown out a large portion of the lares and penates collected during nearly thirty years of marriage, including a number of pots and pans. I tend to hang onto everything just short of forever, but when I finally make up my mind to clear away the extras, I do it with reckless abandon. When I set up my San Diego kitchen, I felt like someone just learning to cook. I was about to drown my sorrows by going on a binge at a big kitchenware store, when I got a bid from a pots-and-pans-and-more manufacturer to do a cookbook for the company. A meeting where ideas and terms were straightened out concluded with the inevitable "Be sure to send Mrs. Townsend some of our product for testing."

I awaited eagerly the large crate, possibly even two crates, that would soon arrive. But not in my wildest imaginings did I anticipate a truckload. Not one covered casserole, but nine, in all sizes, in round, square, and oval shapes. Two eight-inch pie plates, two nine-inch, two ten-inch, plus a broad assortment of quiche, flan, and pizza pans. Skillets both round and square, in small, medium, large, and jumbo sizes. Saucepans galore, dutch ovens ditto. Rectangular baking pans in all possible combinations of dimensions, three each for good measure. Cookie sheets, four assorted-size roasting pans, jelly-roll pans, soufflé dishes, a dozen round ramekins and a dozen square ones, a dozen each of three sizes of custard cups, four

—count 'em, *four*—double boilers, and much, much more, including a couple of things I had to have recourse to the catalog to identify.

With the help of a visiting sister-in-law and a neighbor who dropped in, my husband and I eventually got all the new things stowed away. Their temporary quarters included, besides kitchen cupboards, a bedroom bookcase (we left the books in their boxes for the time being), the spaces under two beds, the shelf in the guestroom closet, a portion of the linen closet, and a set of shelves my husband hastily put up in the kitchen, which didn't get painted until the cookbook was finished. The quantity was excellent, if a bit overwhelming, and the quality was even better. These were top-of-the-line utensils, and I had a ball every minute of testing in them. When the cookbook was finished, I made the usual call, asking to what address I should return them, and was told, "Oh, please don't. What would we do with them? Just enjoy them."

In one blow, so to speak, I had written another cookbook and restocked our kitchen. Enjoy them? I certainly have, and still do. After some judicious weeding-out and presenting to friends and helpers, relatives and neighbors, I still have sufficient pots and pans so I shall never have to buy another.

KEEPING THE WHEELS TURNING

Perhaps all this food-related activity will give you ideas of going into a food-related business. Many cookbookers have moved from producing books to producing the foods with which their books are concerned. I've never taken this step (when I weary temporarily of cookbooks, I move to editing or to some other kind of writing), but I know a number of people who have and can offer a little advice gleaned from their experiences.

To what fields do cookbook writers turn? There are several.

Produce Your Specialties, in Your Own Home

Apparently it is not difficult to work up, through the grapevine or word-of-mouth route, a list of regular customers who will be delighted to buy your products, perhaps on a once-a-week basis. Another way to go is to locate a small restaurant (or two) or a fancy-foods specialty shop to sell your wares.

CAUTIONARY NOTES. Produce, at least to begin with, foods that do not spoil readily, such as cakes, cookies, and/or breads. Be sure to check to see if you need a license, a health-department inspection, or anything else to allow you to legitimately carry on such a business. Set prices sensibly: figure out, to the last grain of salt, what each of your products costs to make (don't forget cooking energy) and then double, or double-and-a-half, that figure to reach a price you will charge your customers. Don't take on more customers than you can comfortably cope with—fifteen cakes a day can be a lark the first week, an unbearable burden by the third.

Start a Restaurant

If you have always wanted to own a restaurant, and if you are reasonably young, have a body bursting with energy and a head bursting with ideas, this may well be the right time.

Besides energy and ideas, you will need money: rent will have to be paid on the premises you use, appliances and equipment bought or rented, and food purchased. And don't fool yourself that you can manage the whole business on your own—nobody can be the cook, the waitress, the cashier, the scullion (general cleaner-upper), the janitor, and the dishwasher all at the same time, no matter how tiny the establishment.

CAUTIONARY NOTES. First off, you must have a license. (If you propose to serve liquor, you will need a second license, one for which, in many places, you may have to wait as long as five years unless your spouse happens to be the mayor.) Consider your present lifestyle: Is there anything in it that will prevent you from spending as much time as the restaurant will require, particularly at first? If you have a spouse, is he or she in total agreement with you about the project? Is there anything in your way of life that may prove a stumbling block? (For example, there is a pretty, airy breakfast-and-brunch-only restaurant near our house, serving excellent food, providing efficient service, enjoying a good business. But the proprietors are Seventh Day Adventists, and close the restaurant on their sabbath, Saturday. Saturday, unfortunately, is the biggest eat-breakfast-out day of the week.)

Start a Catering Business

Some kinds of catering can be done from your home—hot and cold hors d'oeuvres for a cocktail party, for example, or small sandwiches and cakes for a tea, or punch and cookies for an informal reception, or sweet rolls and beverage for a morning coffee, or several handsome sweets plus a cheese and fruit platter for a dessert-and-coffee party. From your own home you can even cater a small dinner, of a size you would give yourself, or a buffet for a small crowd. But be aware that catering of this sort does not fill the big need for which the profession exists: supplying food for large groups of people. There is no way that a lone person can cater a sit-down dinner for 350, or an elaborate wedding reception for 500, from her own home. If you can confine yourself to reasonably small parties, and make a good job of them, you can probably work up a repeat clientele and earn a living. Otherwise, forget it, or be prepared to go into the business in a big way—which means spending big money.

CAUTIONARY NOTES. Depending on your city ordinances, you may or may not need a license. Also, be aware that most people expect caterers to supply more than food—tables, chairs, table linen and napkins, china, glassware, flatware, floral arrangements for the tables, liquor and bar supplies, and a professional-type bartender. All these except the floral arrangements can be rented, but you will have to develop good, reliable sources.

Work as a Cook in a Restaurant, Resort, Camp, Whatever

If you are inordinately fond of cooking, this may seem, at first blush, a dandy idea. It isn't. In the first place, unless you can offer a certificate of graduation from a good hotel-restaurant-catering school, you're going to be at the bottom of the pecking order in any kitchen, doing the hardest, least-rewarding jobs, scurrying around like a demented chicken, at everyone's beck and call. You will work long hours for short pay. If a resort beckons you because of the amenities—beach, fresh air, and so on—I can only hope that you will have an hour off now and then to enjoy them.

CAUTIONARY NOTES. Unless you are a devout masochist and/or have the stamina of a bull elephant, pass this idea by.

OTHER WAYS TO GO

Suppose, for a moment, that you never get to bask in the delights that I have enumerated here: the publication of your book and the concomitant enjoyments and benefits. Suppose, in other words, that you can't sell the darned thing. Then what? If you have followed along with me, by the time you reluctantly conclude that you can't—at least at present—sell that first book, you should be well along with work on your second.

Come to a halt for a moment and try to view that first book objectively. Is the basic idea really a good one? Is the organization of the book up to standard? Is the writing up to par? Did you do your market research poorly—that is, does your book very nearly duplicate others in print, with little to distinguish it? Or does it have something new to recommend it? Is it the only one of its kind and therefore a "must-have"? Have you sent it to good-for-cookbooks publishers, rather than those who never, or very seldom, publish cookbooks? Is the manuscript neat and professional looking? If you can answer those questions truthfully, and find the book not wanting in any way that you can discover, there are several avenues open to you.

1. Ask a professional critic (for a fee) to advise you. There are a number of possibilities here. Approach a teacher of writing at an accredited college or university; that person should be able to critique the manuscript him- or herself, or point you in the direction of someone who can. Or seek out a cookbook writer, one who has had at least two cookbooks published, and ask for help. To find such a person, inquire of one of the writers' organizations, such as P.E.N., or your local Society of Writers and Editors—they may not call themselves exactly that, but there is such an organization in almost every town of any size. Or ask the food-section editor of your local newspaper to recommend someone to you. Such people may not be the world's foremost critics, but what they will do is bring a fresh perspective to the work.

2. Try the small presses. The very small ones, particularly those in your area, shouldn't be overlooked. One of the editors in such a publishing house may find your book exactly to his or her liking. No, you won't make a lot of money—probably no advance and a rather miserly royalty—but you will be published. At the same time, make an all-out effort to sell a couple food-oriented articles to magazines. With the book and the articles, you will have better credentials to present along with a proposal for your second book, when it is ready. Also, once in a while —not very often, I admit, but once in a while—a big publisher will see a small-press book and be so intrigued

with it that he will buy the rights and republish it. One of the books that has been on the *Publishers Weekly* best-seller list for the better part of six months arrived there by just such a route, so it does happen . . . sometimes.

3. Try to find an agent. I know, I don't really believe cookbooks need agents. But by now you may very well disagree with me. At least, no more than anyone else, agents don't wish to waste their time; because the agents' commission is on the *sale* of the book, they are unlikely to take on a book they don't believe they can sell. Also, agents are quicker—and likely to be more frank—to tell you what ails the book than editors are.
4. Keep on slugging. Keep on tidying up the manuscript, retyping the query letter, and sending out your material. There are a great many publishers out there, and all you have to lose is your postage.

There is one very important thing not to do: *Don't turn to a vanity press.* These subsidy publishers, as they prefer to call themselves, are in business to turn a profit. That's all right—so is everyone else—except that the way they make that profit is to publish a book for less than they charge you to have it published. If you deal with a vanity press you will, indeed, end up with your book in type and between covers. In fact, you'll probably end up with huge piles of them getting mildewed in your basement or garage, far more than you can give away as Christmas presents if you live to be a hundred. And you'll have, as well, a substantial hole in your wallet.

All right, you vow to avoid the subsidy presses. But how about self-publishing? Although I am assured that this route can be successful, I find it hard to believe. What I *do* believe: Unless you have the proper aggressive, self-realizing personality for it, unless you can spend a great deal of time promoting the book and a great deal of energy seeing to its distribution, unless you know a great deal about the nuts and bolts of publishing so your book won't appear to have been thrown together by an ungifted amateur, and unless you can afford to lose a substantial amount of money, put the temptation of self-publishing behind you. It's nervous-breakdown territory. Under some circumstances, self-publishing can be as maddening as the vanity press route. Consider the San Francisco man who self-published his science-fiction novel. He offered to donate five hundred copies to the local public broadcasting station for a fund-raiser auction, but was politely refused. After several other such offers and refusals, he finally dumped the books in the parking lot of the famous Cow Palace and set them afire. "It's not easy, being a writer," he told the firemen.

Although I don't believe that recourse to a vanity press is ever called for, there are some situations where self-publishing is a legitimate way to go. One is the community or fund-raising cookbook, which we'll deal with at length in the next chapter. Another might be the situation of a recent widow whose husband, although he spent all his life manufacturing plumbing fixtures, wrote poetry as a hobby. The widow might very well decide to self-publish his verses to give to family and friends in remembrance of him—a worthier cause, perhaps, than that of the widows who blow their insurance on trips around the world. Closely allied is the firm whose elderly and respected founder dies, and which may want to put out a history of the company, to give to employees and customers, in honor of him. But that's about it, so don't be tempted.

MAKING PUSH COME TO SHOVE

The foremost thing in a writer's mind, either while waiting for his or her sold book to be published or while waiting for an unsold book to be sold, should be to keep on working. I know —pep talks are easy to give and hard to take. But unpublished writers become published authors by writing. And writing some more. You, too.

Chapter Eight
Special Circumstances: Community and Fund-Raiser Cookbooks

One of the ways to raise money favored by many organizations is a cookbook written, produced, published, and sold by members. It doesn't always fulfill its purpose—that is, it doesn't always raise money and may, indeed, lose a bundle. But if it's produced by dedicated people who are willing to work hard and to proceed with reasonable caution, the book can be a great success and a great pleasure as well.

Almost any sort of organization can—and has—put together a community cookbook. A large company, for example, that manufactures windmills or cane tips or elevators or anything else in no way connected with food and cooking may decide to put out a cookbook of its employees' favorite recipes to use as a goodwill gesture for new customers or to give at holidays. In such a case, the budget may be reasonably liberal, and the company may hire a cookbook professional or two to oversee the job. At the other end of the scale may be the women's guild of a small church, hampered by a bare-bones budget and a lack of know-how, but spurred on by determination and a talent for hard work. Between these two poles lie a number of other kinds of would-be cookbookers, many of them groups of adjuncts to larger entities, such as the docents of a museum or the auxiliary of a lodge. Membership of such groups is composed largely, or solely, of women who are homemakers or at most employed part-time: women, that is, who have sufficient leisure to devote themselves in part to charitable or other volunteer work in addition to their homemaking. Most of these women are cooks, some of them probably very accomplished cooks. And that constitutes the jumping-off place for a community fund-raiser cookbook.

THE MEETING WILL PLEASE COME TO ORDER

As I believe I remarked earlier, anything that is ventured by a committee already has two strikes against it. I don't mean that the project will be impossible, but it certainly will be difficult. Even if the committee members are dear friends at the beginning of the venture, a few of them are likely to be blood enemies by the time it is over. Projects of this sort bring out the aggressiveness in potential bullies, aggravate the shyness of the timid, and generally exacerbate the less desirable qualities in everyone while masking their naturally sunny dispositions, if any. Am I suggesting that you forget the whole project? No. I'm not saying that a committee cannot put out a cookbook, but only that it is difficult. That it can be done is proved by the number of such cookbooks (fifteen thousand, one authority says) that appear each year. Not only do they appear, but a large percentage of them prosper, encouraging their committees to bind up their wounds and start putting together Son of Cookbook.

All right, enough of this throwing cold water—one of the less desirable qualities that mask my otherwise sunny disposition. It's time to get started.

To begin with, a temporary committee should be appointed to explore the possibilities of putting out a cookbook. It is simpler to do this than to attempt to put together a permanent cookbook committee from a meeting of the entire membership, without any preliminary study of the situation. The temporary committee should read books and articles on the subject of fund-raiser cookbooks, work up a list of possibilities for membership in the permanent committee and particularly candidates for the editor, who will be in complete charge of the project, and the art director–designer, on whose shoulders rests responsibility for the appearance of the book and for the smooth running of the mechanical aspects of preparation. The committee can also make suggestions as to what sort of cookbook it should be, based on an informal survey of the membership and a knowledge of the members' lifestyles. A family cookbook? A book of foods for entertaining? A book to teach children to cook? A collection of desserts or of main dishes or of snacks and appetizers?

At a meeting of the full membership, the committee's findings should be presented, and decisions made based on them. Executives and committee heads should be elected or appointed, according to the usual procedure of the organization, and committees formed to attend to every phase of book production.

There are two valid ways to go about forming committees, with arguments pro and con for each. Each committee chairperson, after election or appointment, can be allowed to choose the people she wants to compose her committee. In favor of this method: The committee head will choose people she likes and knows she can get along with, people she knows will be workers, not slackers. Against the method: The people who have been doing most of the work for the organization for years will find themselves once again doing all the work; the clique system can cause hard feelings among nonclique members; some people well qualified to work on the project may be overlooked. The second method is to elect or appoint not only the committee chairperson but all the members of each committee as well. In favor of this method: It is likely to be more fair than the first system, and to place on the committees people who are skilled in the work they will be asked to do. Against the method: The chairperson of a committee may find herself saddled with a sloth or two, or worse, with someone to whom she has barely spoken for the last six months and whose ideas and ideals are diametrically opposed to hers.

Here is a rundown of workers necessary to get the book together from start to finish, and the jobs for which each group should be responsible:

1. *Editorial committee.* The chairperson of this committee will be the editor of the cookbook; it is necessary that every member of each committee, as well as the general membership of the organization, understands that the editor is in charge, that she has the final say, that she is the last court of appeal. A second important member of this committee is the designer, who, if at all possible, should be an artist, equipped with all an artist's skills. Each will need three or four people to function as assistants.

2. *Finance committee.* This group will control the budget and keep the books for the project; should okay every pro-

posed expenditure before it is made. Will also request and receive bids for typesetting and paper, printing and binding, and decide, in conjunction with the editor and the designer, which of these vendors to use. Sets up bank account; pays bills.

3. *Recipe committee.* Responsible for gathering all the recipes, eliminating duplications, sorting and categorizing recipes, giving them a preliminary reading, checking to be certain all elements are in place in each recipe.

4. *Testing committee.* Chosen from among the best cooks in the organization, these people must be willing and able to devote as much time as necessary—and it will be quite a bit—to testing the recipes that are submitted for use in the cookbook.

5. *Typing committee.* Chairperson organizes, assigns work to a collection of very good (and cheerful) typists, each of whom has unlimited access to a good typewriter.

6. *Copy-editing and proofreading committee.* Responsible for grammar, spelling, punctuation, and syntax before the manuscript is sent to the typesetter and after the typesetter has returned it.

7. *Distribution and fulfillment committee.* Makes all the arrangements for the sale of the book; sets up displays for sale of book in local bookstores, supermarkets, food specialty stores, craft shops, and the like; arranges for book sales at community carnivals, fairs, and so on; enlists assistance of other clubs and organizations in town to push sales of the book; arranges for (free) announcements about the book on community affairs programs of

local radio and television stations and in newspapers and other community publications. Handles mail and phone orders for the book.

All committees, including distribution and fulfillment, should begin to function at approximately the same time. However, before they start work as units, a general meeting of members of all committees will give rise to a number of questions and will also, it is to be hoped, find answers to them.

EARLY DAYS, EARLY WAYS

If the method of financing the book was not addressed by the general membership of the organization at the time it was decided to put out a cookbook, this should be the first order of business. If you can't see your way clear to paying the bills, all bets are off and you should shut up shop before you open it.

True, you expect to sell the book and to make enough money to pay for its production and also to provide a tidy profit for the organization. However, you can't start making money on the book until a book exists. If you can stomach a tired old piece of economic truth, you must spend money in order to make money. You will probably be able to find a printer who will wait for a part of his fee until the book begins to generate a profit, but—unless he happens, by lucky chance, to be an affluent fellow who is also a relative of one of the members—he will not wait long for all his money, nor should he be expected to. He, too, will have bills to meet: typesetting, unless it is done on the premises; paper, which is expensive; binding, unless it is done on the premises, and even if it is, cover stock, binder's board, and other binder's supplies will have to be purchased.

Where will the money come from? Perhaps it already exists, in the organization's treasury—indeed, a tidy bank balance at the time of the last treasurer's report may have been the catalyst that got the whole cookbook project underway. Or you may be able to borrow from a local bank, credit union, savings and loan, or the like; just be aware that this money will have to be repaid, and on time, and that you will have to pay interest—probably anywhere from 12 to 18 percent—on the money. Better, one of the members, or the spouse or some other relative of one of the members, may be in a position to lend you the money. Again, it will have to be repaid, of course, but the terms may be more lenient and the interest lower. Or you may be able to find some other source willing to get the book on its financial feet. But until you know where the money is coming from, don't forge happily ahead under the impression that the Lord will provide. He won't. He has too many really important problems to handle, and you shouldn't even for a moment entertain the notion that this project is worthy of divine intervention.

Once financing is assured, you can turn to other considerations. "How much are we going to charge for the book?" is one of them. Surprisingly, this is not a question to which an answer can be found at this preliminary organization meeting: it must wait until the finance committee has done part of its work, collected bids or otherwise arranged for the production of the book, so that you have at least a rough idea of what it is going to cost. I could tell you several horror stories here, all of them relating to a low price being set and printed on the cover before someone thought to do a little simple addition and multiplication. You must, of course, decide on a cover price for the book that is higher than the unit cost of production—that is, a total of all expenditures divided by the number of books produced. And when I say cost, I mean *entire* cost—office supplies, postage, gasoline for the station wagons of the people who will deliver books to the various arranged-for outlets, *everything,* as well as the big bills for paper, printing, and binding. If you have borrowed money, don't forget repayment plus interest. Once you figure out the unit cost, double or triple it to get a reasonable cover price.

Another question: "What is the book going to look like?" That, too, must wait on the finance committee's findings. A good printer will offer you a lot of options: perfect or spiral or comb binding; a single- or two- or four-color cover; various grades of paper; monotone or two-color in the printing of the body of the book; and more. Which options you choose will depend on what you feel you can afford. But don't try to settle the question until you have bids; if you decide on a particular kind of binding, a certain standard of appearance, and then find that you can't afford them, you'll never feel quite the same enthusiasm for your cookbook again.

Two matters that you can settle at this meeting are the general contents of the book and the amount of time you'll give yourselves to produce it. To make the first choice, ask yourselves questions about your community. Is it a suburb, the kind where a great deal of entertaining goes on? You might do a cookbook of foods for parties—perhaps a Saturday Night and Sunday Morning cookbook. Is your climate so delightful that everyone spends time outdoors? Think about a cookbook for barbecues, patio dining, picnics—foods for all sorts of alfresco eating. Is the area very much family-oriented?

Consider Family Feasts or Fast Family Feasts. Whatever theme you choose, make certain that it will have the widest possible appeal, and therefore assure the widest possible sale.

As for a time frame, you should be safe if you decide that the book will go on sale two years from the date of conception. If this strikes you as too long a gestation period, please believe me when I say that everything, *everything,* will take at least twice as long as you think it will. To pace yourselves, set interim deadlines: Date when all recipes must be in, when all recipes must be edited and typed, when copy-edited manuscript must go to the printer. When you have settled on a printer, he will give you a set of deadlines on the work he will be concerned with: when the first proof will be in your hands and when it must be returned, when second proof or page proof will come to you and when it must go back to him, when the book will be on press (he will probably want a couple of people, such as the editor and the designer, to be present, but don't you allow the entire cookbook committee to troop over and get underfoot), when it will go to the binder, when finished books will be ready for distribution.

Speaking of distribution, you must make arrangements, in advance, for the books to be warehoused. Obviously, they can't be fired off in all directions at once; a large number must be held to fill mail and phone orders, to resupply outlets that have sold their original allotment, and so on. Bear in mind that books are bulky and heavy, and that dampness is their enemy, when you choose a place to store them. Can't they be left with the printer? Perhaps, but probably not; small printers have small places of business, and need all their room for their own supplies.

Another matter for the agenda of this all-committee meeting: A call for recipes must be sent out. Members of the various committees will wish to offer recipes of their own, no doubt, but the general membership of the organization must be canvassed for recipes as well. Being businesslike about it from the start will save a lot of time and trouble later on. Make up a recipe form similar to the one shown on page 199, which leaves spaces to be filled in for all pertinent information: the donor's name, address, and phone number; the recipe category; recipe title, ingredients, and method; recipe source. The form should also carry a disclaimer saying that if duplicate recipes are submitted, the first one received will be used (this speeds everyone up), that only the most suitable recipes will be chosen (if you say "best" you'll get a lot of flak), and that recipes will be edited so that presentation will be uniform throughout the book (saves you from a barrage of howls of "What have you done to my recipe?"). Make certain that you set a deadline for receipt of recipes, that it appears on the form, and that you abide by it in spite of all the pleas and excuses you will get.

RECIPES, IN AND OUT

As the recipes come in, they should be checked by the recipe committee to make certain all blanks are filled in, and then sorted by category. If there are duplicates or near-duplicates, clip together for the editor's attention. The recipe committee should also check each recipe to see that all items in the ingredients list are used in the method, and all items called for in the method appear in the ingredients list. This checking should be careful and thorough, because sins of omission occur in these circumstances more often than in any other. When a mistake is found, the donor of the recipe should be called at once and the error rectified, to save the editor and the testing committee grief later on.

Now it is the editor's turn, assisted by the good cooks of the testing committee. Every recipe should be read carefully. This time around you are not looking for errors, but for acceptability. Does the recipe sound appealing—as if it would produce good flavor, pleasant texture, attractive appearance? Does it belong in the category in which it has been placed? Or somewhere else? Or does it not belong in the book at all? Is the title in keeping—not too cute, not too long, not unrelated to the recipe, consonant with the tone you are setting for the book?

Now divide the recipes, placing those with which you are delighted in one place, the doubtfuls in another. Have the "delighteds" photocopied; give one set to the testing committee, one to the copy-editing committee to hold. The testing committee should then start doing their thing. Divide this first batch of recipes among the members, preferably giving each one a variety rather than all soups, all desserts, and so on. Each recipe should be accompanied by a brief test form, stapled or taped to the recipe, on which the tester fills in her name, date of testing, and comments on the recipe results. If the results are unsatisfactory, but the recipe still sounds like a good one, have it tested again by someone else; if it still doesn't work, put it among the discards. If, after all the first-choice recipes have been tested, there are not sufficient to fill the book, move on to testing second-choice recipes to fill the gaps.

Testing should begin as soon as a reasonable number of recipes has arrived; reading, editing, and testing should go on, in an even flow, from that point until deadline. After

RECIPE FORM FOR COMMUNITY COOKBOOKS

CALL FOR RECIPES!

Dear Member: As you know, The Docents Society of the Old Masters Museum is preparing a cookbook for sale to our members and friends. Your cookbook committee would be delighted to receive recipes from you for possible inclusion in the book. No recipes will be considered that are not submitted on this form. Send us up to five recipes, each on a separate form. DEADLINE IS APRIL 22—NO RECIPES WILL BE ACCEPTED AFTER THAT DATE! Send or bring your recipes to Jill Featherberg [address and phone number]. Thank you for helping to make this project the success we all know that it will be.

Submitted by [name]__________________________

Address________________________ Telephone________

Source of recipe____________________________

Recipe title________________ Makes____ servings

Cooking time________ Temperature_______ Pan(s)________

Ingredients (in order of use; please specify exact measurements as well as can and package sizes):

Method of preparation:

USE OTHER SIDE OF PAPER IF NECESSARY. PLEASE TYPE, OR WRITE OR PRINT CLEARLY. NOTE THAT ONLY RECIPES SUITABLE FOR THE BOOK WILL BE CONSIDERED, AND THAT ALL RECIPES WILL BE EDITED FOR THE SAKE OF CONFORMITY.

deadline, and after testing is complete, it's time for the editor and her committee to make a final decision: Which recipes will go in the book, which will be discarded? If you are short of acceptable recipes in some categories, send out a second call.

Recipes that have received the testers' and the editor's blessing should now be turned over to the typing committee, each member of which should be supplied, by the editor, with a dummy recipe to follow for form and spacing. (See such a dummy on page 55.) Recipes then go to the copy-editing–proofreading committee for careful checking and tidying. Remember that everything on each recipe page can come back from the printer just as is—misspellings, typos, unfortunate phrases, punctuation errors, and all—so this is a very important step. (See page 201.)

Meanwhile, the editor should be seeing to peripheral material: general introduction, finished title and introduction for each section, history of the organization if it has been decided that this should be included, any special features that will appear in the book, and the title, copyright, and contents pages, as detailed on pages 89–93. These materials should be given to the copy editors for checking as well.

One member of the copy-editing team should be designated as indexer. As each page of manuscript is copy-edited, she should make an index card for that recipe, carrying recipe title, category (such as main dish), and chief ingredients. For the time being, file the cards alphabetically. When the entire manuscript is complete, pages should be numbered straight through, from one to whatever, and any other page designations crossed out.

Now have the manuscript in its printer-ready entirety photocopied. Why? Because you don't want to find out the hard way that manuscripts can get lost. Believe me, I remem-

COPY EDITORS' AND PROOFREADERS' SYMBOLS

There is more in heaven and earth	Move down
There is more in heaven and earth	Move up
]There is more in heaven and earth	Move in
[There is more in heaven and earth	Move out
¶ There is more *or* There is more	Start a new paragraph
There is is more *or* There is is	Delete (remove) and close space
There is mo re in heaven	Close space
There is morein heaven	Insert space
There is more in heaven	Insert quotation marks
Theres more in heaven and earth	Insert apostrophe
There is more in heaven and earth	Insert 1-em dash(es)

☐There is more in heaven and	Indent 1-em space
There is more in heaven=and=	Insert hyphens
There is mØre in heaven and	Reduce to lowercase (lc) letter
There is more in heaven and	Elevate to an uppercase (UC) letter
There is more in heaven and in heaven⊙	Insert period
There is moer in heaven and earth	Transpose (2 letters)
There is more in heeavn and earth	Transpose (3 letters)
There is in more heaven and earth	Transpose (words)
There is more in heaven and earth, Horatio, than	Align margin
There is more in heaven and earth,	Insert comma
There is more in heaven and earth 2	Print as superior (earth²)

There is more in heaven and earth^3	Print as inferior ($earth_3$)
There is more in heaven and earth	Set as italic (or, if text is in italic, set underlined word in roman (rom))
There is more in heaven (and earth)	Insert parentheses
There is more in heaven and earth	Set as small capitals (sm caps)
There is more in ~~heaven~~ and earth	Stet (restore crossed-out material)

ber as if it were yesterday the time I learned that horrendous truth. I was working full time, commuting nearly two hours a day, keeping house, and now and then writing a freelance story or article to help with mortgage, alimony payments, child support, and assorted bills. It was the holiday season, with all the extra time-and-temper demands the holidays always make; nevertheless I managed to finish—on time, but barely—a story that was due at the editorial office on December 27.

By a stroke of good luck, my typist was going to have a quiet Christmas at home and was willing to spend part of it typing. I delivered the manuscript to her, gave her the phone number of my husband's parents, where we would be going to Christmas dinner, and took off, leaving the typist, her husband, and two kids happily opening presents in a welter of ribbons and wrapping paper and empty boxes. By the time we arrived at the elder Townsends', the typist had already phoned three times. I called her back, to hear her hesitant, anguished explanation of how her super-neat husband had gathered up all the mess of papers and boxes and taken them out to the incinerator. Somehow he had managed—in the manner of throwing out the baby with the bath water, I assume—to incinerate my manuscript as well. I leave you to draw your own picture of the ensuing bedlam, and to profit by the moral of the story.

So, your manuscript is ready for the printer? Well, not quite. It needs to be marked up, a job for the designer—alone, or if she is not sure of herself, with the printer's help. The purpose of the mark-up job is to tell the typesetter in what type face and what size to set all the various elements of the manuscript: front matter, introduction, section titles, section introductions, recipe titles, ingredients lists, methods, and all the rest. (This same process is gone through for a trade-book manuscript as well, done by a member of the publisher's art department or by the freelance artist who has been hired to design the book.) This is somewhat tedious, but not a difficult job, as the designer and the printer should long since have decided on types and type sizes.

The printer gives the manuscript to his or an outside typesetter, and presently back it comes, all neatly (I hope, and so do you) set in type. The editor will read the proof, and the copy-editing and proofreading committee must read it with great care and concentration, in a quiet, interruption-proof place. The best proofreading practice employs two people: One (the copyholder) reads the manuscript aloud and the second (the proofreader) reads and corrects the proof. If it has been returned to you as page proofs—single pieces of paper, each of which carries the material that will occupy a single page of the book—it should be read not only for errors but also for widows (less than a full line at the top of a page or column) and orphans (one short word, or the final portion of a broken word, at the bottom of a page or column). If the proof has come back as galleys—long, narrow pieces of newsprintlike paper—besides being read it will have to be cast. While casting is increasingly being handled by computer-pagination programs, in situations when it is done in-house, it is, again, a job for the designer. He or she will either count lines, spaces, and half spaces (the safer way) or use a page-length template (faster, but not as accurate) to divide the proof into pages or, if there are two or more columns to a page, into columns. Where the bottom of each page or column falls, the designer will mark the proof with the page number, like this:

> When completely cool, cover and store
> at room temperature up to three days.
> -----------------p 28

If the page is broken into columns, the column designation will also appear:

> When completely cool, cover and store
> at room temperature up to three days.
> -----------------p 28 L

> making a well in the center of the dry
> ingredients, add eggs, oil, and vanilla
> -----------------p 28 R

The marked proof should be returned to the copy-editing–proofreading committee for a final go-round: a last look for widows and orphans, and a careful satisfying of all page references—that is, "see page 00" should now be turned into "see page 56" and so on throughout the book.

If the proof is in galleys, the cast should be copied, along with all corrections that will have a bearing on the index, onto a clean set for the indexer, who can now go to work. If in page proofs, an extra set should be supplied for the indexer. The corrected proof should be returned to the printer. When the printer sends you second proof with corrections made, he should also return the old set. Now the procedure is gone through again, this time with the copyholder reading from the old (first) proof, and the proofreader reading and marking the new (second) proof.

A caution that bears repeating: When a book is in proof is not the time to have second thoughts. Proof exists so that errors can be corrected, not so everybody can have a whack at rewriting the book. Do that, and your bill from the printer will far exceed his original bid and rise to astronomical heights that would cripple any budget.

ONCE MORE, WITH FEELING

All that has been said before about trade books applies to community cookbooks as well: how to approach the non-recipe material, proper form for recipes, and all the rest. Keep the information in earlier chapters firmly in mind, because it is just as true of your effort as it is of the professional writer's trade cookbook. Sure, you're amateurs, but that is no reason for your book to look like, or read like, the product of a bunch of people who had no idea what they were doing.

It is sometimes suggested to community cookbookers that, if the budget will possibly allow, they hire a professional or two to help put the book together. If you can afford only one person, the advice continues, that one should be an editor.

I beg to differ. I think that the professional, if one is hired at all, should be a designer or an art director (these are semi-interchangeable terms, and anyone who is professionally one or the other can perform the necessary duties on your book). I say this in spite of the fact that I have functioned as an editor a good part of my life, and even in spite of the fact that editors and art directors are often at odds over who should make what decisions and who is treading on whose professional toes.

I believe that anyone who is reasonably intelligent and reasonably well-educated (and a reasonably good cook, to boot) can transform herself into an editor for a fund-raiser cookbook, particularly with the assistance of a good art director. But it is impossible to make a good art director out of a sow's ear. It is a job for which considerable talent is needed and, more important, considerable training. It is too much to ask of a printer that he wave his magic wand and transform a novice into a book designer overnight. So opt for hiring a designer if you can hire anyone. If you can't, try to find someone among the organization's members who has had some art training at some time, or who has worked in a print shop. From there on, lean heavily on the printer, ask questions if there is anything at all that you don't understand, and forge ahead. You'll make out. Hundreds of others have made out just fine on the wing-and-a-prayer principle.

DESIGNING DONE HERE

Knowledgeable professional or fear-filled amateur, the art director–designer of a community cookbook must work closely with the printer. In the publishing business, a trade or paperback book house may have its own presses—although very few do, nowadays—or may choose among a large number of printers whose sole business is producing books. Such books are generally printed on web presses (called that because feed-in from gigantic rolls of paper resembles a spider's web) and are run by computer. But your choice for a community fund-raiser will likely be a local print shop, perhaps the one that prints the town's weekly newspaper as well as advertising flyers, wedding invitations, business cards and letterheads, and the like. Such a shop will probably be equipped with one or several job presses, on which shortrun material such as flyers is printed, and a flat-bed press. Shaped, not surprisingly, like a large bed, this monster makes an unconscionable amount of noise, smells wonderful or dreadful depending on whether or not you enjoy eau de printer's ink, is equipped on one end with a feeder to supply it with paper, on the other with a folder that grabs the printed sheets and folds them into book-size bundles, and a dryer—to dry the ink, but not completely—in between. Some flat-bed presses are new and do their work with reasonable efficiency and comparative quiet; others break down with dismal regularity, smell sickeningly of leaking gas—the dryer is gas-fired—make a noise past tolerating without earplugs, and should long ago have been put out to pasture. When you have spent a good deal of time standing by such a press, it takes another good deal of time to stop twitching in rhythm with its nerve-shattering SLAM-rattle-rattle-rattle, SLAM-rattle-rattle-rattle.

The shop may also be equipped with a Miehle Convertible or other press capable of printing four-color book or magazine covers on good stock, or the printer may farm out such work of that kind as comes his way. In the center of the shop there will be at least one stone—a soapstone- (or, nowadays, often plastic-) topped island—and a light table, an area topped with glass and lighted from below. Around the edge of the room will be wooden holders for various kinds of type —"California cases," they are called—and in one corner a linotype machine, looking a bit forlorn because it is seldom used nowadays. Near it will be one or several computer typesetting machines, clean and quiet and unsmelling—and looking like the intruders that they are.

Presiding over all this there will be a shop foreman, a capable-looking man wearing a denim or leather apron and perhaps a square, folded-paper printer's cap on his head. His arms may wear several ugly scars, souvenirs of the days when linotypes sometimes spat boiling hot, liquid lead at their operators; those scars will mean that he is an old-timer and knows his business.

This foreman is the link between the outside world—you and your cookbook—and the inside world of printing. Cultivate him. If he is your friend, all that has to do with typesetting, printing, and binding the book will go well. If not, the road to getting the book out will be filled with potholes and detours. Above all, don't disdain him because he is smeared with ink and grease and works with his hands. If you do, he will swiftly prove to your chagrin that he is a whole lot brighter than you are.

THE PERFECT BLENDSHIP

The friendship between the art director and the printshop foreman is a crucial one. The foreman can smooth the way for the art director, who, taught by the foreman, can smooth the way for the rest of the cookbookers. If he or she doesn't already know how, the foreman will teach the art director how to cast a manuscript to determine how much material will go into so many pages when typeset in the style agreed upon.

Suppose that the book is designed to accommodate 4 recipes in 2 columns per page, and that the agreed-upon bulk is 224 pages. Besides recipes, the book will carry the usual front matter and index, a brief foreword by the president of the organization, a 4-page history of the organization and its work, an introduction by the editor (telling how the book came into being, how recipes were acquired, etc.), 12 section-opener pages that will carry the section titles and introductions—but no recipes—a 2-page glossary of cooking terms, and an index. Here you go:

224 pp. in book
– 4 front matter
220
– 5 foreword and history
215
– 2 editor's introduction
213
–12 section openers
201
– 2 glossary

199
– 6 index
193 number of pages on which recipes will appear

193 × 4 = 772 recipes, @ 4 recipes per page

If this were to be a trade book or a commercial cookbook illustrated with full-color pages of food photographs, that number of pages would also be subtracted before the total number of recipes could be calculated.

This, the cookbook committee will suddenly realize, is a lot of recipes. A whale of a lot of recipes. Perhaps, if the organization is large, that many recipes—good ones, nonduplicates—will turn up. If not, what to do?

Back off. But you can't do it haphazardly. There are two ways to go:

1. Cut the number of pages (which will also cut the per-unit cost). But don't assume you can cut any number that comes to mind. Books are printed in blocks of pages called signatures, and each signature is made up of a set number of pages; in books, the number is usually 16. (But check with the printer—it can be 24 or 48 or, indeed, any wieldy multiple of 8, depending on the press; magazines are often printed in 8-page signatures.) So, if you are going to cut pages, you must cut 16, or—two signatures—32, or whatever number the press can accommodate.

2. Redesign the page. Decide to set the type in a different width (perhaps you will have to go to another type face for the sake of good looks) so that the page will accommodate 2, instead of 4, recipes. With one stroke you have reduced to 386 the number of recipes required. And the book will be both better looking and easier to read.

Anyone (it is to be hoped) can add and subtract, and those two are sufficient to carry you through. Quadratic equations can come in handy to editorial and art-department workers, though. Suppose you're editing a book that has been designed to 256 pages at 36 lines per page. The author has been asked to revise two chapters; they come in at considerably greater length than they were the first time around. A quadratic equation can tell you in a moment how many lines must be added per page to remain at a paging of 256, or how many pages must be added to retain 36 lines per page, or how much must be cut to retain both the original lines per page and the original page count. Square root? Well, if you know the square root of 256 you will also know that there will be 16 signatures in a 256-page book made up of 16-page signatures; useful for, as a simple example, placing color pages in a book which will have a wrap-around color fall—that is, color available at the beginning and end of each signature (i.e., will *wrap around* the signature). In a large publishing house, these are things you needn't bother about; in a small house, you may be called upon to juggle a couple of equations between washing the windows and sending out the mail.

MOVING RIGHT ALONG

If you, the cookbook committee, keep in mind that this book of yours is just as important, and requires an equal amount of effort and dedication as any other, you'll produce an effort you can all be proud of. The recipes should be just as well tested, just as properly organized and worded, as those in any trade or commercial cookbook. Ditto the nonrecipe material. Anything worth doing is worth doing well. That's tiresome, isn't it? Boring. Yup—boring but true.

If you have a theme—old-fashioned recipes, fish and shellfish, salads, whatever—stick to it. This is an area in which community cookbookers tend to stray. Mrs. Fanspeed's orange torte, absolutely delicious and known far and wide in the community, does not fit the fish-and-shellfish theme. You know that everyone (including, particularly, Mrs. Fanspeed) is going to be disappointed if you don't include it. What do you do? One way is to be merciless. Leave it out and stick to your theme.

However, a sneaky end-run is possible in circumstances like these. Include menus—not just one, to accommodate that torte—but a number of them. No one is going to expect you to suggest a menu composed totally of fish and shellfish, so you can slide in other recipes by this route. For example, suggest a menu for a warm-weather bridge luncheon, such as:

Spring Scallion Soup
Scallop and Snow Pea Salad
Sesame Monkey Bread
Orelia Fanspeed's Orange Torte
Coffee

This gives you the opportunity not only to give the recipe for the salad, which by definition has a place in the book, but also for the soup, the bread, and the torte. You have, in one swoop, mollified Mrs. Fanspeed and added variety to a cookbook that might otherwise seem a bit on the dull side.

Be careful in choosing themes, by the way. If you live in Backwater, Iowa, where the only local fish are sunnies from the pond, forget fish and shellfish. If you live in a suburb populated with upwardly mobile young marrieds who are struggling with mortgages and car payments, don't offer a book loaded with truffles, caviar, *tournedos de boeuf,* and gravad lax. Keep in mind, too, how swiftly food fads come and go; don't fill your pages with raw fish that may be out of style—and so, out of mind—by the time the book appears.

Remember, too, that today's people, particularly young people, are aware of good nutrition and into fitness: a book consisting totally of high-calorie, empty-nutrient dishes isn't going to go over well. And be aware, as you all must be in your own homes, that meals are lighter nowadays than they once were. Don't offer menus and recipes for seven-course dinners, not even if the dinner giver is supposedly entertaining Prince Charles and Lady Di. Plan carefully, think before you act, stick to sensible ideas, and you'll make out just fine.

I SAW IT IN THE PAPER, SO IT MUST BE TRUE

Somewhere in the early, planning stages of your community cookbook, someone is sure to come to a meeting armed with clippings of ads she has taken from newspapers and magazines. One such ad reads:

PUBLISH YOUR OWN COOKBOOKS
Groups Earn from $50.00 to $93,000.00

Quite a financial span there! Another ad offers:

FUN RAISER
$60.00—$600.00—$6000.00
and more!
Sell Your Groups Very Own Cookbook!

The lack of apostrophe might give one pause even if the rest of that ad didn't. Another one has this to say:

RAISE AS MUCH MONEY AS YOU NEED FOR
YOUR CHURCH, SCHOOL, TEAM, OR CLUB
Publish Your Own Cookbooks!
With Favorite Hometown Recipes!

These ads, and others like them, go on to explain—but not very fully—that all you must do is submit recipes, and the advertiser will accomplish all the rest. You will have ample time to pay, they say; one offers ninety days, another promises that you need not pay for the cookbooks until after you have seen and sold them. "Economic recovery is here," says one, "now is the time to prosper." Most of the ads hold out tempting goodies—four-color covers, plastic comb bindings, "sixty pages of basic cooking information, many of them in full color."

Do these ads sound tempting? In a way they are. Who would not be tempted by a little-work/big-profit offer? But think about it. The covers are preprinted in large numbers, and need only to run through a press for a stamping of your organization's name. That sixty-page section is also preprinted, and will be the same as the sixty-page section in dozens of other organizations' cookbooks. You will find that the advertisers are not nearly as liberal with terms, as accommodating about waiting for their money, as they are made out to be in the ads. And some few of these offers are outright scams.

But the main objection is the fact that when your organization decided to do a cookbook, it was to be *your* cookbook. Most of these mass cookbook producers are located where you are not. Once you have bundled off your recipes, you will have no control over your book. It will look and sound like dozens of others, because it will *be* like dozens of others. You will have paid nearly as much as, or more than, you would have paid at home for a cookbook that appears to be a mass-produced item, because that's exactly what it is. You won't sell as many as you would of your own book, partly because it will look commercial, partly because you have not bled and died putting it together. So think twice, and then again.

YOU'RE ALL INVITED

To launch your cookbook, give a party. Serve foods made from recipes in your cookbook. Stage it in your organization's quarters, or in someone's garden, or in the church parish house. Invite everyone—members and their friends, people important in the community. And, of course, sell everyone a cookbook.

Have a bake sale, or a food bazaar. Feature foods from the cookbook, and offer small but tempting samples (take care that the foods are not perishable, or that you have adequate refrigeration). Stage a gifts-from-the-kitchen jamboree at holiday time. Offer a service by which a member of the committee will (for a fee, of course) prepare any dish in the cookbook, in any quantity, for noncook readers to serve at a party. Make sure the cookbook is available at bookstores, markets, specialty shops, shopping malls, and recreational facilities. Be certain there are books waiting to be sold in your own meeting place and, if your organization is church connected or an auxiliary of a larger group, that there are copies of the book, nicely displayed, in the vestibule or meeting hall. Give each member a quota of books to be sold. Enlist your young people to canvass neighborhoods door to door.

These are only some of the ways to sell fund-raiser cookbooks. Just keep constantly in mind that in order to raise funds books must be sold, so seize every possible opportunity. Once the book is printed you are by no means finished with it. That's only the beginning.

Putting together a community cookbook can be both fun and hard work. Have a lot of both, and a good sale as well, so you'll soon have to go back to press for more copies.

Chapter Nine
Ornamental Frosting: Food-Photography Sessions

Perhaps not in connection with your first book, but certainly some time along the way if you stay in the cookbook business, you'll be called upon to participate in food photography for cookbook illustration. These sessions can be a pleasure or a pain, depending on the congeniality factor of the people involved and the suitability of the studio and its equipment.

Food photography takes place every day, all over the country. But the two chief locations are the East Coast, particularly New York City, and the West Coast, particularly Los Angeles. Because of the differing situations in the two areas, conditions under which pictures are taken differ as well. In New York, space is at a premium; every single real-estate inch counts, because every single inch is extremely costly. Unfortunately, you can't take pictures—food or any other kind—in a closet. Photographers need broad floor areas and high ceilings to do their work and ample space in which to store their bulky paraphernalia. Add to those requirements a place for a darkroom, plus offices, reception area, rest rooms, dressing rooms, and, with food photography, at least one well-equipped kitchen, and you're talking about a studio whose monthly rent could blow your socks off.

This is why New York studios tend to be in low-rent districts. There are no parking places, of course, so you must arrive in a taxi, wrestle the equipment you've brought out to the curb (New York taxi drivers being what they are, yours will remain behind the wheel, chewing his cud, during this operation), step over or prod aside a couple of drunks in the doorway, and, your arms full, climb several flights of inadequately lighted stairs while dodging the creep who makes you an indecent proposal on the first landing and the purveyor of hot jewelry who is lurking halfway up the second flight.

In sharp contrast is laid-back California's largest city. Los Angeles has all the charm of a cold boiled potato, and when the smog rolls in you feel as if each breath might well be your last. But what Los Angeles lacks in personality it makes up for in space. Angelenos think of themselves as living in a crowded place and complain of the high cost of real estate, but they just don't know whereof they speak. A Los Angeles photographer's studio I know well occupies a roomy, airy building with a high-ceilinged ground floor and a lower-ceilinged second floor; there is an ample parking lot at one side of it. The first floor has a handsome reception area with offices and darkroom and rest rooms behind it; on one side of this core are two kitchens, each boasting everything a cook could ask, with a shooting area between. On the other side is a third, even larger and plusher kitchen, a small permanent set of various kitchen components used for shooting, an empty shooting area, and a cloakroom. All across the back lies storage space.

The second floor houses extra equipment, plus a sort of orderly flea market composed of every possible sort of prop for food photography: set after set of china, glassware, hollowware; cooking utensils of every description; tablecloths, place mats, and napkins in a wide assortment of colors and materials; odd decorative pieces, such as bird and animal statues, Chinese figurines, a collection of fans, ceramic fruits and vegetables, and much more; candle holders from single- to many-branched candelabra, along with appropriate candles in a selection of colors. But why go on? Ask and ye shall receive—anything you might want is there. Better still, someone knows exactly where to find it.

In New York, most props must be borrowed, rented, or purchased as they are needed, simply because there is no place to put them when they are not in use. After they've done their job, the borrowed or rented ones must be carefully packed up and returned—delivery services love to have photographic studios as accounts—and there is a certain amount of maneuvering to claim the purchased ones. The client—that is, the publishing house or, if it's a commercial cookbook, the food company—has first dibs; after all, a charge for props will appear on the client's bill. If the client says no, a genteel free-for-all ensues among the author, the art director, the photographer, the stylist, the cook, and anyone else who happens to be on the spot. The author has the right of primogeniture, so to speak, and the others offer an assortment of excuses to support their claims: The stylist says that the object is, by happy coincidence, an exact match for one she owns, and she'd love to have a pair; the art director's wife's birthday is next week; the cook's first cousin once removed is about to be married, and so on down the line.

CAST OF CHARACTERS

When I say "characters," I mean it. Each of these people has, to put it kindly, his or her small eccentricities.

The Photographer

To begin with, the photographer. He may be as temperamental as a matinee idol or as down-to-earth as a lumberjack, but there will be something in his makeup that requires kid-glove handling. One I worked with many times seemed to be just about perfect—businesslike, efficient, loaded with talent. However, as everyone who worked with him quickly learned, it was necessary to come to a grinding halt about once an hour and tell him how wonderful he was. A simple "My, what a fine photographer you are!" was not enough. What was required was for the head honcho present—usually the author, me—to clasp her hands on her heaving bosom and deliver a three-minute paean of praise. This was, as you may well imagine, a swift pain in the derriere. But if it was overlooked, the photographer would grow progressively poutier, finally flinging himself off the set to slam into his office and not be seen again that day. But he was so good (and his prices were so good, as well) that clients put up with him.

Other photographers I have known had various little peculiarities. One was drunk a good deal of the time, and although we hid his bottle whenever we could, finally had to be crossed off our list. Another, seemingly normal and blessed with otherwise impeccable taste, was crazy about artificial flowers. Not the handsome—and expensive—silk or porcelain ones, but dime-store-variety plastic flowers, wearing ugly, unflowerlike colors, so stiff they appeared embalmed. He kept sneaking these monstrosities onto the set, and I kept sneaking them off. Sometimes he won, sometimes I did, until I announced that the game was over: Thereafter, I would okay no bills for photographs in which artificial flowers appeared. Threatened with a wound in his most vulnerable spot, his wallet, he backed down.

Another photographer was allergic to onions, which posed no problem when we were doing desserts, but caused considerable uproar at other times. It is difficult for a photographer to be at his best when his eyes are streaming and he's sneezing eight to the bar.

Typically, the photographer's staff consists of an assistant, a receptionist, a brawny soul who wrestles backdrops, and a gofer. If a series of how-to pictures is to be done, there will also be a hand model. And if film is processed on the premises, there will be a printer. All of these are generally pleasant people, their only fault being that, if the cooking staff is not on its toes, they will eat up all the food before it can be photographed.

The Stylist

If there is going to be food photography, it follows that there must be a cook. Sometimes it is the cookbook's author. Sometimes it is a home economist—or several—who specializes in cooking for photography and is hired for the occasion. And sometimes it is the person designated, with capital letters, as the Stylist.

Here again, as with studios, there is dichotomy between East and West. In California, the stylist (known more formally as the food stylist) prepares the food for photography, with the aid of an assistant or two, one of whom is usually the author. In consultation with the author, the photographer, and the art director if one is present, the stylist decides in what dish(es) the food will be placed, against what background, and in general in what manner the set will be dressed.

The photographer's assistant digs out appropriate dishes, utensils, and other props from the storeroom and assembles the set while the food is being prepared.

New York, as it is about everything, is rather more elegant about the styling process. In the first place, the stylist usually does not cook—for all I know, she can't. Well before the shooting dates, she (sometimes, these days, it is "he," but women stylists are still in the majority) is presented with copies of the recipes that will be used, along with notes from the author concerning anything out of the ordinary that may be required and a description of what the finished appearance of the food will be. The stylist, who spends a good deal of her time engaged in some women's favorite pastime, shopping, knows what's new in her favorite stores and where she can find anything she needs. She makes lists and sketches, designing the set for each picture, and then sallies forth to borrow (first choice), rent (second choice), or buy (if all else fails) the props that will be needed.

Stylists—the New York brand, at least—are a breed apart. One of whom I was particularly fond was the only child of wealthy parents. Although she could have spent her life sitting on a silk pillow eating bonbons, she hated that idea, decided to put her good taste and flair for design to better use, and became a stylist, an exceedingly good one. The only problem was that when you called her for a job (stylists are for the most part freelancers) she was likely to be in the Aegean on someone's yacht or at Ascot for the races. A serenely beautiful brown-eyed blonde, when she did manage to work she was invariably collected at the end of the day by a young man driving something like a Ferrari or an Astin-Martin or by an older one in a chauffeured town car. She was great, the best stylist I've ever used. When the going got tough, she tied a dish towel around her elegantly clad waist and pitched in with the dog work, peeling and chopping and mincing and slicing with the best of us. A graduate of a finishing school where she had been taught to walk like a queen with a heavy book on her head, she was the one who carried intricate dishes to the set, picking her way gracefully and safely through the mine field of ropes, electric cords, generators, and other hazards.

Another New York stylist of whom I was fond was British, getting along in years. With her upper-class accent, her black dress touched with white at the throat, she was the very picture of a gentlewoman in reduced circumstances, forced to support herself as a governess. Her taste was excellent and (probably because nobody dared say no to such a classy lady) she turned up some fantastic props. She was very reserved, and it was a long time before I learned that the reason she collected bits and pieces of food in a big plastic bag throughout the day was that she had, in the British manner, a whole menagerie of pets at home. With so many little mouths to feed, she was obliged to scrounge and scavenge wherever she could.

She was constantly thirsty but, because I was taking medication that made my mouth and throat dry, so was I, and I thought nothing of it. Liquor in that studio was never broken out until after the day's final shot, so nearly everyone drank soft drinks, with which one of the refrigerators was well stocked. But the stylist didn't like soft drinks, and so prepared a tall glass of ice water for herself in the morning and kept it replenished all day. When she learned that I shared her aversion for carbonated beverages, she prepared a like glass for me each day, and we sipped away in well-bred austerity while the others slurped their bright-colored liquids. All was well, until the time I took a deep drink of my ice water and reeled back, spluttering. I had mistaken the stylist's glass for my own, and hers held vodka, not ice water.

"Oh, sure," the photographer said, when I mentioned it later. "I've known it for a long time. Quite a few studios bar her. But I feel sorry for the old girl, so as long as she continues to do a good job, I'll continue to hire her. Yeah, that's my vodka she's drinking, but it's your chicken and beef and whatnot she's eating—she doesn't have any pets, you know. Live and let live, I say."

Stylists of the West Coast are not nearly so exotic. Hair tucked back and aprons snug, they go efficiently about their business—which is, largely, cooking. They prepare handsome foods, the photographer shoots them, and that's that.

Invasion of the Outlanders

Required for a good food photograph are a good cook and a good photographer, plus assorted supernumeraries: some kitchen help to do the preliminary preparation of food, a dishwasher (human, please—mechanical ones always have the dish you want that very minute tucked inside them and are in the middle of the wash cycle), and a couple of general fetchers and carriers. What is definitely not required is a large and critical audience.

But with certain cookbooks, most often commercial ones, you get such an audience willy-nilly. You get a home economist—or, if you're particularly unlucky, several of them—from the food company's test kitchen. Some of these ladies are great. They roll up their sleeves, button their lips, and pitch in. But others just stand around and carp, and when they get tired, they sit around and carp. Sometimes they decide, in midstream so to speak, that a recipe should be changed. Or a garnish redone. Or a sauce added. Or the cook fired. Or the author shot.

Along with the home ecs from the food company comes the marketing manager or, worse, the vice president for marketing. He brings his secretary, in case she's needed to take notes. He also brings his assistant, in case he needs someone to order around. From the advertising agency that handles the food company's products comes an account executive, followed by his retinue of an assistant, a copywriter or two, an art director, and a home economist (or several, for good measure) from the agency's test kitchen. Next, from the public-relations organization that publicizes the company's food products comes an account executive (whom you will be unable to distinguish from the ad agency's ditto), followed by *his* assistants, copywriters, home ecs, and (I sometimes think) the office boy and window washer. Once in a great while one or another of these people will bring along a wife and children, who have been just dying to see how the pretty pictures are made. One female account executive brought her tiny apricot poodle, which yapped without letup all day and which was, I swear, equipped with an innerspring that allowed him to leap lightly up on anything less than seven feet high, usually into something like a bowl of pea purée or a nest of spun sugar.

Some of these people are pleasant, although hardly self-effacing—that doesn't go with the profession. Some are downright awful. But good or bad, they add up to quite a number of bodies milling around and breathing. What do you do? Nothing. You bear in mind that come hell or high water the client is always right and go grimly about your business.

TASTY MORSELS AND SNEAKY TRICKS

In New York City, as you have undoubtedly noticed if you live there, food in the supermarkets, and even in such specialty shops as uptown greengrocers, tends to look a bit down at the heel. You get used to tearing off the outer leaves of lettuce (the ones with the most nutrients) and throwing them away, to refreshing celery and parsley in ice water in the vain hope of restoring them to their original crisp perkiness, to poking and smelling the meat and fish suspiciously, to checking the thermometer in the freezer.

On the other hand, convention holds that food for photography ought to be as near perfection in appearance as possible. What to do? In New York, order supplies from one of the three or four markets that specialize in beautifully photogenic food. The cost is astronomical, but the results are worth every penny. If you order eight avocados, eight unblemished ones will arrive, each in exactly the same stage of ripeness as the other seven, all exactly the same shape, all exactly the same size. The center-cut pork roast will be a model of piggy pulchritude, firm and white fleshed, elegantly trimmed, exactly the weight ordered. Lamb chop and crown roast and rack bones will be neatly frenched, all to the same measured depth, and wearing ruffled panties. Even so unremarkable a thing as a can of pepper will be without dent or flaw, will have been carefully washed and dried, ready to have its picture taken if such should be its destiny.

All this beauty is a bit daunting, making you feel as if you should ask the avocado's permission before peeling it. Considerably more daunting are the prices: the avocados three dollars a piece at a time when they were selling for forty-four cents in the common people's stores; the roast twenty-three dollars, working out to just under four dollars a pound, at a time when such a piece of meat was less than four dollars for the entire roast in a very good butcher shop.

But as well as daunting, such food is exhilarating. It is a real pleasure to work with—especially when you remind yourself that someone else is paying the bills. The saddest time comes when you must do something to that lovely food that you know will render it unfit to be eaten. A set of do-or-don't rules exists that governs the shooting of food pictures to be used in ads (all part of the "truth in advertising" campaign), so few of the traditional dirty tricks are used in that field. But in food photography for cookbooks anything goes, and often does.

Some of these tricks are innocent and harmless. Apples and pears are polished to within an inch of their lives. Uncooked foods are sprayed with water or a glycerine-water mixture, to make them look dewy fresh; cooked foods are treated to a spray of light oil to make them look succulent. Serving dishes are packed with marbles or crumpled foil before the fluffy mashed potatoes or whatever are piled on top to save the cook from preparing all those potatoes; woe betide the disher-upper who allows an aggie or a bit of silvery paper to peep through. Knives are heated in order to cut ice-cold butter into neat, uniform pats. Meats are painted with a mixture of oil and gravy strengthener to give them a brown glister. Yellow food coloring is stirred into custards that don't look eggy enough, red into cherry pie filling that's a bit pale, amounts of gelatin are doubled or tripled to assure that the salad or dessert will stand tall when unmolded, meringues are given extra back-bone with marshmallow cream.

I once caught a photographer gravely retouching with acrylic paint an eggplant that apparently didn't look eggplanty enough to suit his taste. White eggs are given a bath in coffee if brown eggs are required and there are none on the premises. A drop of food coloring gives milk a creamlike color, and if more body is called for as well, some nonfat dry milk is stirred in. I spent considerable time one morning attaching with florists' wire pretty radishes from one bunch to the better-looking leaves and stems of another bunch. At the same time, armed with a steam iron and thick pressing cloth, the home economist I was working with was getting the wrinkles out of some grape leaves, while the stylist brought some discolored mushrooms back to pale perfection with a sponge bath of Clorox.

Sometimes a total substitution is called for. One photographer is firm in the belief that coffee, no matter how long and strongly brewed, never looks like coffee in photographs, and substitutes a mixture of his own made of lots of Kitchen Bouquet, a little water, and *one* drop of laundry bluing. Is tea called for? Use a little less Kitchen Bouquet, of course, and hold the bluing.

Vegetables are seldom cooked more than a minute or two, and are often simply blanched in boiling water; treated this way, the vegetables look fresh and inviting and lose none of their color. Ignoring the recipe, meats are often cooked at very high heat for a much shorter time than they should be, leaving them handsomely brown and shapely; if the meat is pork, this makes the cooks nervous, fearful that someone will come along and slice off a piece for a trichinosis sandwich. Another habit that gives the cooks fits is the adding of darkroom hypo to beer, which gives it a splendid, stand-up head but also renders it lethal. Another is the flambé system worked out by one photographer, who does it with lighter fluid—gorgeous, long-lasting flames, licking over deadly Cherries Jubilee.

Some foods are difficult to photograph, and ice cream is at

the top of that list. Almost all foods for photographing are prepared in duplicate: one dish to use as a stand-in while set and lights are given a final adjustment, the second reserved for the actual picture. But when the dish is ice cream, triplicate—or, safer, quadruplicate—is the order of the day. The ice cream is spooned into prechilled dishes, hastily garnished if that is required, and hustled into the freezer for an overnight firming. The next day it goes under the lights, where it reduces itself to melancholy puddles in no time flat.

A New York cookbooker some time ago invented a fake ice cream that looked exactly like the real thing, even to the texture of the part that had touched the scoop. She could produce it in any flavor, and it stood up like a little trouper under the lights. We found out, in time, that this wonder was based on Crisco, but nobody could determine what the other ingredients were, and our efforts to duplicate her feat always looked like Crisco instead of ice cream. She confided in no one, and when I left town the secret was still hers alone.

On one occasion, when we were due to photograph a baked alaska the following morning, the home economist and I made four of them. We wanted to be absolutely certain that we could take the shot next day, which was the last day of shooting on that project. They were handsome, those alaskas, tall and snow-capped. Each of us—the home ec, the photographer, the cook's assistant, and I—took one alaska each and marched off to the freezer. Three of us arrived safely, but the home ec, normally sure-footed as any gazelle, turned her ankle and slipped. One down, three to go.

Next morning, the photographer decided that he'd get a stand-in alaska from the freezer. After all, he pointed out, he had more experience at broken-field running across the studio than the rest of us. Sure, he did—but this time a coiled electric cord reached out and tripped him. Two down, two to go. "Let me," said the home ec. "I can't possibly have two accidents in a row." And she was right. She ferried the alaska across the studio without incident. "See?" she cried triumphantly, making a dramatic, sweeping gesture—and knocking number three off the table. Three down, one to go.

"Fix me up a stand-in of just meringue," the photographer suggested. "I'll make do with that, and then we can shoot the last alaska and get this nightmare over with."

So we did, and he did, and the moment of truth arrived. "My turn," I said grimly, and went to get the final alaska. I opened the freezer. It held a number of goodies, but no baked alaska. Could we, in the midst of our travail, have lost count? No. Anyone capable of preparing a baked alaska must be capable of counting to four, using her fingers if necessary. Okay, it must be in the other freezer, an older, less reliable appliance. I opened it. No alaska. "Where the hell *is* it?" I bellowed to the studio at large. A moment's silence. Then, "Oh—I remember." That was the cook's assistant. "It's in the stainless-steel one."

The stainless-steel one was brand new, handsome, efficient looking. But unfortunately it was a refrigerator, not a freezer. I opened it, knowing what I would find. And there it was, spread over the pretty serving plate, a puddle of goo. Four down, none to go.

WHAT'S FOR LUNCH?

In some studios it is the custom to send out for lunch or even, if important clients are on hand, to order a catered lunch, on the theory that the cooks are too busy to scrounge up a meal.

But in other studios that the cooks will provide the noontime spread is an accepted custom, and speculation concerning the day's provender begins early in the morning. "Let's shoot the cakes first," says the photographer with a sweet tooth, "so we can have them for lunch." The stylist eyes the assorted greens, tomatoes, cucumbers, avocados, and such. "We won't be needing these after the noon break, will we? There's turkey and ham from yesterday in the fridge, and there's sure to be some cheese, too. If you'll make that great anchovy vinaigrette of yours, we can have a big chef's salad." The printer pauses to inhale with ecstasy as he passes the stove. "Oh, boy! Cioppino! Listen, if you don't have wine for it, I'll run down to the corner and get a bottle of Bull's Blood."

The last remark arises from the fact that the cooks often shortcut by omitting ingredients that don't affect the appearance or consistency of the food: Wine is left out of many dishes, flavoring extract "forgotten" in cakes, cookies, and puddings. Sometimes too much, or a wrong ingredient, is used: The ratio of flour to shortening in pie crust is increased, which makes it less prone to crumbling and breaking, but also renders it tough as a motorcyclist's jacket; burned, rather than lightly browned, flour is used in making gravy, giving it excellent color and an emetic flavor. So "Can this be eaten?" is often heard.

Everyone in a studio knows the number-one rule: Don't eat anything without first asking the cook. Sometimes the item has been rendered inedible. Sometimes it simply hasn't yet been photographed, and cooks get very cross when they go to arrange a tempting plate of brownies and find nothing but crumbs in the cookie box.

By the end of a shooting, in spite of all the lunching and morning coffeeing and afternoon teaing and in-between snacking that has gone on, the cupboards and refrigerators and freezers will be crowded with food, and must be emptied in readiness for the next wave. There are two choices: Take it home or throw it out. As it would be sheer, wasteful madness to throw out a couple of pounds of butter, a half-wheel of cheddar, a loaf of my special pâté, four pints of heavy cream, three boxes of out-of-season raspberries, salad makings sufficient to feed an army, two standing-rib roasts, two loaves of the cook's wonderful stovepipe bread, nearly a full peck of potatoes and the same of white onions, eight artichokes that traveled all the way from California for their brief moment before the cameras, two bottles of Zinfandel, three of Chardonnay, two of Pinot Noir, and one of Bull's Blood, to mention only a few of the treasures, a great jockeying for position ensues.

Anything the client wants, the client gets—after all, the client foots the bills. Then the pecking order is: home economist, author, stylist, photographer, cook's assistants, photographer's assistants, dishwashers, and gofers. (If you have people from a food company, an ad agency, and a PR firm on the premises as well, protocol can get a bit sticky.) Often, common sense takes over. The stylist, to whom the artichokes should go, doesn't like artichokes and trades them off for a pound of butter. The vegetarian photographer wants no part of a roast, and exchanges it (he's a lacto-ovo vegetarian) for a loaf of bread, half the cheddar, and two pints of cream. Although the cook's assistant isn't really in line for the pâté, she's giving a party tomorrow night and is awarded it anyway. The printer has a raft of kids and so is sent home with dozens of assorted homemade cookies that aren't truly his due. Generally the portioning-out process works quite smoothly, although now and again someone, feeling done out of a fair share, gets a bit huffy.

P.S. Bull's Blood? It's a hearty Hungarian red wine, full

flavored and richly colored, which stands up assertively to the rigors of cooking.

WHO GOES THERE—FRIEND OR FOE?

As in any walk of life, in food photography—indeed, in cookbooking in general, as well as all forms of writing and publishing—you meet a great many delightful people and a few peculiar ones.

I could write a book entitled *Home Economists I Have Known.* In common with any other group on the planet, they range in appearance from the strikingly beautiful to the downright homely, in disposition from cosy to vicious. From those points, the circle of differences widens. I've known many who were splendid cooks, but I knew one who couldn't cook worth a cent; that would have been acceptable, if slightly odd, if she had been a home economist specializing in a field such as clothing or consumer protection, but her specialty was food —which regularly, every day, she reduced to inedibility.

Another had two cats, which she hauled along to all food photography sessions. They arrived in their carriers, but were released as soon as the studio doors were closed. If you know cats, you also know that they can, with ease and grace, get anywhere they make up their one-track minds to go. I yield to no one in my love for cats and all the other furred and feathered creatures, but each has his place and that place is not the kitchen when food is in preparation. I object to a cat who sticks her foot in the cream jug so she can lick it clean, to a cat who samples the just-unmolded salmon mousse, leaving a series of dainty bite marks, to a cat who steals (and hides only she knows where) the striped bass that was about to be stuffed, to a cat who with neatness and dispatch removes every speck of frosting from a cake.

"My," said the home ec after this last disaster, "who would've thought that Fluff-Wuff would like chocolate frosting?"

"Who would have thought the old man to have had so much blood in him?" I replied balefully.

The lady, who may not have been up on her Shakespeare but who recognized a threat, however veiled, when she heard one, packed up her cats and went home.

On one occasion, a high-fashion photographer acquaintance of mine telephoned to ask if I would prepare a number of very elegant dishes in his kitchen, to be photographed along with a number of equally elegant evening gowns. "I think it's a delicious concept, don't you, darling?" he asked.

Coward that I am, I agreed. The next day I ran over in my mind the layout of his studio. I could not recall that the amenities included a kitchen, so I dropped in on my way to another job. The kitchen, which he showed me with pride, turned out to be a small closet equipped with a couple of beat-up pans, a two-burner gas plate, and an elderly toaster oven. When I explained that I would be hard put to it to produce anything edible, let alone elegant, he became quite angry. We threw a couple of epithets back and forth, and I left. At a party months later, he remarked stiffly that he owed me an apology. He had, although he couldn't imagine why, been unable to find anyone else willing to take on the job.

Ah, well, it takes all kinds. In spite of the off-beat characters, food photography is fun. A good way to earn a living if you're so inclined, certainly a good sideline for a cookbooker who wants to get away from the typewriter for a time.

A FUNNY THING HAPPENED ON THE WAY TO THE COOKBOOK

When I first started working in food photography, neatness not only counted, it was All. Everything was painfully tidy, squeaky clean. Each item to be shown in the picture was carefully aligned with every other item, and all were set down precisely, foursquare to the camera. The food itself had to live up to these high standards, of course. Sauce was carefully spooned on, to occupy no more than a quarter of the food it garnished, and no drop must be allowed to stray from those bounds. Bread must be cut in measured slices, each not a whit thicker or thinner than its companions. Dozens of eggs were broken to get two or three divided equally for a process shot (food in the process of being prepared). Crates of strawberries were sorted through to find ten that measured up. Salads were built by hand, leaf by leaf of greenery, slice by slice of vegetable, to give them an air of studied nonchalance; shredded cheese was strewed on piece by piece to achieve a strictly regimented carelessness. Crumbs were anathema, crumbles a sin, and the tiniest breakage, such as at the edge of a pie shell, could earn you forty lashes at the mast.

The pictures that resulted from all this blood, sweat, and tears looked good. They looked too good to be true. Obviously, nobody but a squad of experts giving their all could produce such unsullied magnificence. How could one home cook live up to those standards? Most home cooks were afraid even to try. Others compared the results of their best efforts with the cookbook photographs and, shedding oceans of tears, never darkened the kitchen door again.

So it finally dawned on us that we were being too picky, and everything—the food and the people who were preparing and photographing it—relaxed. Not that sloppiness is condoned, nor slipshodness tolerated. But food in today's cookbook pictures looks as if the home cook can hope to achieve its duplication. It looks friendly, not snooty. It looks as if it had been prepared in a kitchen, not a laboratory. It looks, in short, as if you would dare to eat it, even enjoy it.

Another trouble with food photography in the bad old days was the size of the picture's field. The camera backed off and shot not only the food in question but large areas surrounding it. If those large areas were left blank, they looked peculiar, so we filled them with everything that came to hand: vases of flowers, candlesticks and candles, little—and not so little—figurines, baskets of fruit, baskets of bread, coffeepots or teapots and their accompanying cups and saucers, sauceboats, small ashtrays, dishes of salted nuts, china and silver and crystal in ostentatious display. Finally someone, unable to locate in a picture the food that the picture was all about, cried, "Enough, already!"

Once again we backed off. For a short time we had a spell of austerity so great it was virtually poverty: one piece of plain food sitting on one plain plate in the midst of a vast nothingness. Then photographers began sneaking up on the food, coming closer and closer, until each hill and valley of a slice of bread showed that it had been cut with a serrated knife, each pit and nodule on the surface of a chop looked like a severe case of acne, frosting on a cake looked like the hills and craters of the moon. There were no areas of nothingness surrounding the food, because the surrounding areas were out of the picture. In fact, once again it was hard to decide what the picture portrayed, not because you were so far away from it, but because you were so close to it.

Today, things seem to have reached a happy medium. Everyone has realized that the whole point of taking a picture of, say, a lamb stew, is to render it seeable, identifiable—and so that the viewer will say to him- or herself, "That looks great. Think I'll fix a nice lamb stew for dinner tonight. We haven't had one for ages."

LET'S HEAR IT FOR COOKBOOKERY

If you are equally comfortable at the typewriter and in the kitchen, and if the products of your efforts in both areas are outstanding, you have the makings of a good cookbooker. Once you surmount the obstacles of writing your first cookbook and getting it published, you're safely on your way.

Writing cookbooks isn't by any means a start-to-finish breeze, but very few things worth doing ever are. There are highs and lows along the way, as well as a reasonable amount of level, jog-it-easy ground to keep you from being either depressed or manic for too long a stretch. As does any other way of life you might choose, it has rewards, both monetary and ego satisfying. There are punishments in the form of long stretches of time when you'll be completely convinced that no one will ever buy anything from you again, interspersed with periods of activity so frenzied you'll yearn to go work in the coal mines as a relief from the pressure.

But all work has its rhythms, and sooner or later you'll learn to adapt, to relax and go with the flow, to count the dry spells as time in which to think and to research, the frantic flurries as a game you know you can win because you've won before and will win again.

Even if the prospect of a lifetime of testing recipes and putting them down on paper doesn't appeal to you as the ideal career, think of it this way: Cookbooking is an excellent way to get started on a general writing career, or one in publishing. You'll learn a lot—not just about chiffon cakes and crown roasts and deep-fat frying, but also about research and editing and transferring ideas from your brain to paper. Best of all, you'll learn a great deal about self-discipline, a trait that will stand you in good stead whatever you do.

So don't be timid. Get started on that cookbook of yours. And when the going gets rough—as indeed it will—remember that Irma Rombauer's *The Joy of Cooking* was once a community fund-raiser cookbook in St. Louis. That's a thought to inspire any cookbooker to new and greater efforts.

A Library for Cookbookers

Whatever you write, it is impossible to do a decent, acceptable job without recourse to reference material. Depending on your set of mind, you may have a few useful volumes or sit, grinning happily—as I do—in the midst of so many books there's little room for anything else in the house. Even the most sure-of-themselves writers need something to fall back on when they hit a snag, something to reinforce them in case of doubt, something to give its blessing to their conjectures, something to serve as arbitrator when they are of two minds. Books, that is. Reference books. You cannot survive without them.

GENERAL REFERENCE

A good dictionary. Desk size to keep at hand; also, if you wish, a big, complete dictionary (preferably on a stand, for easy access). The latest edition of *Webster's New Collegiate* is great for the small one, and *Webster's Third New International* (known more familiarly as *Web 3*) for the big one, but any good, accepted dictionaries will serve. Don't stint here—a cheap, slapped-together dictionary is worse than none.

Foreign-language dictionaries. At the least, French. Better, French and German. Better still, French, German, Spanish, and Italian. Plus, if you are going to tackle a foreign cuisine, a dictionary of the cuisine's native tongue—Arabic, Hungarian, Russian, whatever. Make certain that the dictionaries are two-way (French-into-English as well as English-into-French, for example) and that they show all diacritical marks in place. Cassell's are good foreign-language dictionaries, and there are several others.

An encyclopedia. Not an absolute necessity—you can make a trip to the library—but useful. Cookbookers are not as likely to have recourse to the encyclopedia as often as, say, historians or geographers, but you'd be surprised how many times a question comes up that the encyclopedia can answer. For the writer who does not require volumes of the kind of information encyclopedias supply, the one-volume Columbia is a good investment.

An almanac and book of facts. A great many things you want to know in a hurry are here at your fingertips in capsule form. Any of the well-known ones will serve you well, but remember that these are annuals—buy a new one each year; some facts never change, others shift their ground with dazzling rapidity.

A thesaurus. Any version of Roget will do well; I prefer, for ease of use, *The Doubleday Roget's Thesaurus in Dictionary Form.*

Other good-to-have references. A book of quotations; Bartlett is the most familiar. A biographical dictionary. A geographical dictionary. A dictionary of proper names. A dictionary of foreign words and phrases. A manual of style.

BOOKS ABOUT FOOD AND COOKING

There are a great many of these. Sometimes, unfortunately, they don't agree with one another, chiefly on what constitutes a fact, what a theory, what an educated guess. But all are packed with information, some of them offering it in expository form and loaded with anecdotes, others martialing facts and figures in easy-access alphabetical order. No one needs all of them, but a selection can be useful—and can be very good reading, as well.

Some of these books are out of print. Find them at your library or a second-hand bookstore, or ask a book hunter to locate one for you.

Barer-Stein, Thelma. *You Eat What You Are.* London, Ont.: privately printed, 1980.

———. *You Eat What You Are: Glossaries of Foods and Food Terms.* London, Ont.: privately printed, 1979.

Farb, Peter, and Armelogos, George. *Consuming Passions.* Boston: Houghton Mifflin, 1980.

Hillman, Howard. *The Cook's Book.* New York: Avon, 1981.

Jones, Evan. *American Food, the Gastronomic Story.* New York: Dutton, 1974.

Pellaprat, Henri-Paul. *Modern French Culinary Art.* Cleveland: World Publishing Company, 1966.

Rosenthal, Sylvia, and Shinagel, Fran. *How Cooking Works.* New York: Macmillan, 1981.

Simon, André L., and Howe, Robin. *Dictionary of Gastronomy.* New York: McGraw-Hill, 1962.

Tannahill, Reay. *Food in History.* New York: Stein and Day, 1973.

Townsend, Doris McFerran. *The Cook's Companion.* New York: Crown Publishers, 1978.

Trager, James. *The Foodbook.* New York: Grossman, 1970.

Waldo, Myra. *International Encyclopedia of Cooking.* New York: Macmillan, 1967 (two volumes; first consists of recipes, second of information about food).

The World Atlas of Food. New York: Simon & Schuster, 1974.

SOME VERY GOOD COOKBOOKS

These are not, by any means, all the good cookbooks ever written, or even all the good cookbooks now available, but a very small sampling of books by people who know what they are doing and what they are talking about. This list should lead you to others like them, all worth studying and emulating.

Any Craig Claiborne cookbook, with or without Pierre Franey as collaborator.

Any James Beard cookbook.
Any Simone Beck cookbook.
Any Helen Corbitt cookbook (she was extremely inventive).
Any Maida Heatter cookbook (desserts only).
Any of the cookbooks published by *Gourmet* magazine.

American Heritage Cookbook. New York: Simon & Schuster, 1964. Both historical material and recipes.

Anderson, Jean, and Hanna, Elaine. *The Doubleday Cookbook.* 2 vols. New York: Doubleday, 1975.

Hale, William Harlan. *The Horizon Cookbook.* New York: Doubleday, 1968. Both historical material and recipes.

Montagne, Prosper. *Larousse Gastronomique: The Encyclopedia of Food, Wine & Cooking.* New York: Crown, 1961. A phenomenal compondium of basic recipes as well as every variation imaginable.

Rombauer, Irma S., and Becker, Marion Rombauer. *The Joy of Cooking.* Indianapolis: Bobbs-Merrill, 1931 (and followed by many editions).

Tarr, Yvonne Young. *The Farmhouse Cookbook.* New York: Quadrangle, 1973.

PERIODICALS

There are several good monthly magazines concerned largely or solely with food and cooking, each containing many recipes as well as explanatory material, how-to features, and general food information. They include *Bon Appètit, Gourmet, The Cook's Magazine, and Cookbook Digest* (reprints from cookbooks).

There are also a number of monthly or semimonthly cooking and food newsletters; most of these seem to me expensive for the amount of material to be gleaned from them. They are regularly advertised in food and women's magazines; if you are interested, send away for one copy to examine before committing yourself to a subscription.

Essential for the food writer who wishes to include nutritional values and/or calorie counts with recipes is:

Nutritive Value of Foods. U.S. Department of Agriculture Home and Garden Bulletin #72. Washington, D.C.: United States Government Printing Office.

BOOKS AND PERIODICALS ABOUT WRITERS AND WRITING, PUBLISHERS AND PUBLISHING

Books

Books in Print, Paperback Books in Print, Books in Print Supplements, Subject Guide to Books in Print. New York: R. R. Bowker. All are annuals except the supplements, which are issued several times a year.

Literary Market Place. New York: R. R. Bowker. Annual.

Both Writer's Digest Books and The Writer publish a great number of books concerned with various types of writing and with markets for fiction, articles, and books. Note the following:

Burack, Sylvia K., ed. *The Writer's Handbook.* Boston: The Writer, 1984.

Writer's Market. Cincinnati: Writer's Digest Books. Annual.

Writer's Yearbook. Cincinnati: Writer's Digest Books (magazine format). Annual.

Periodicals

The New York Times Book Review, supplement to the Sunday edition of *The New York Times;* may also be subscribed to separately. Weekly.

Publishers Weekly. New York: R. R. Bowker. Weekly.

West Coast Review of Books. Hollywood, Calif.: Rappaport Publishing. Bimonthly.

The Writer. Boston: The Writer. Monthly.

Writer's Digest. Cincinnati: Writer's Digest Books. Monthly.

Many other newspapers publish weekly, bimonthly, or monthly book supplements, which carry information about writing and publishing, as well as reviews of new books and bestseller lists; consult your local library.

SOURCES FOR COOKBOOKS, OLD AND NEW

The Wine and Food Library, 1207 West Madison, Ann Arbor, MI 48103.

Jessica's Biscuit, Box 301, Newtonville, MA 02106.

Kitchen Arts & Letters, 1435 Lexington Avenue, New York, NY 10128. Offers listings of stock by category; i.e. Italian, French, Dessert. Write for a listing in your field of interest and ask to be put on the mailing list.

The three above have very extensive inventories; the Wine and Food Library, in particular, often carries books that can't be found elsewhere. Write to any of them for the latest catalog.

Dover Publications, 180 Varick Street, New York, NY 10014. Reprints old—some long out-of-print—cookbooks, as well as old books in almost any category you can name. Write for a catalog.

Index